WILDFLOWER FOLKLORE

Laura C. Martin

The EAST WOODS PRESS
CHARLOTTE, NORTH CAROLINA
NEW YORK   BOSTON

Drawings copyright ©1983 by
Marguerite Chase Dreyer

Library of Congress Cataloging in Publication Data
Martin, Laura C.
    Wildflower folklore.

    Bibliography: p.
    Includes index.
    1. Wild flowers—Folklore. 2. Wild flowers—United
States. 3. Wild flowers—United States—Folklore.
I. Title.
GR790.W54M37 1984   398'.368213   84-48039
ISBN 0-88742-016-8

Design by Anna E. Birkner
Jacket illustration by Dolores Kennedy
Typography by Raven Type

Printed in the United States of America

An East Woods Press Book
Fast & McMillan Publishers, Inc.
429 East Boulevard
Charlotte, North Carolina 28203

to David and Cameron

CONTENTS

Introduction   7

Blue and Violet Flowers   9

Brown and Green Flowers   65

White Flowers   81

Yellow Flowers   145

Pink Flowers   205

Orange and Red Flowers   221

Glossary   249

Bibliography   251

Index   253

INTRODUCTION

At no other time in the history of our nation has the importance of conservation been greater. Not only is it now necessary that we practice good conservation measures ourselves, but it is absolutely essential that we instill within our children a love and respect for the resources that they will inherit. I know of no better place to begin than with the weeds and wildflowers growing right outside the door. The dandelion, the violet, bedstraw and daisy—there is more to any wildflower than meets the eye, and thus it is from my dedication to the conservation of nature's abundance that, with this book, I introduce you to my friends, the wildflowers.

WILDFLOWER FOLKLORE is a collection of biographies—biographies of the most interesting and well-known wildflowers found in the woods and fields. Many of them are so common they are considered weeds; some are so rare they are classified endangered. The more common the plant is, the more stories, legends, and superstitions it seems to have. From the elegant lady's slipper to the common dandelion, from the rattlesnake plantain to the butterfly weed, from Queen Anne's lace to Dutchman's breeches, each plant is unique; each has its own stories, legends, and superstitions and its own uses for medicine, food, magic, or beauty—in short, each has its own folklore. Learning this folklore is an excellent way to begin to truly know the plants—their nicknames and proper names, their virtues and uses, and their tales and legends. Then when you look at the daisies you not only will think how pretty they are, but you might also pick a few to protect your house against thunderstorms, and when you see the delicate wood anemone, you will think of Anemos, the Greek god of the winds, after whom the plant was named.

The nicknames of the wildflowers are abundant and varied. Many of these names as well as the proper names originated from physical characteristics of the plants. Others are based on the doctrine of signatures, a theory proposed by a Swiss physician in 1657. It suggested that some plants had "signatures" to help man know which herbs and wild plants were useful medicines These signatures were parts of the plant that physically resembled parts of the human body—whatever the plant looked like was what it could cure. For example, since the leaf of *Hepatica* resembles the human liver, it was thought that *Hepatica* had been put on the earth to cure problems of the liver.

Although the flowers and plants have always been appreciated for their medicinal and culinary value, it is their fragrance and beauty that have been prized above all else During the 1600s bouquets of sweetly scented flowers were a necessary part of a woman's wardrobe. These bouquets, used to ward off unpleasant odors common before the days of good sanitary practices, soon

became known as nosegays. In the early 1700s it was popular to communicate by sending nosegays, each flower having its own message. For example, the language of phlox is "a proposal of love" or "sweet dreams," so a girl who received a nosegay of phlox blossoms would be quite flattered. The language of the flowers became quite elaborate, resulting in several dictionaries explaining the meaning of the flowers.

Although some of the medicinal powers attributed to wildflowers have been found to be beneficial, with few exceptions the medicinal and culinary virtues ascribed to these plants were recorded for interest only —not as a suggestion that you defoliate your nearest woods in an attempt to find eternal youth and happiness. However, many of the recipes using the very common plants are fun to make and several are quite tasty. It would do no harm to try them and would enhance your appreciation of the plant to do so. Please be certain of the identity of the plants you use, for there are many poisonous wild plants and many plants that should not be disturbed for the sake of conservation.

WILDFLOWER FOLKLORE will provide you with entertaining reading and a fund of knowledge about the wildflowers. With knowledge comes understanding, and with understanding come the skills and sensitivity to keep our nation's unparalleled resources intact. As you read this book, use it and enjoy it, and above all, enjoy the flowers!

BLUE & VIOLET FLOWERS

MCD
©1983

COMMON NAME: aster
FAMILY: Compositae
GENUS: *Aster*

DESCRIPTION: Since there are more than seventy-five species of aster in the United States, it is often hard to determine the individual species. In general, asters have smooth branching stems that are two to four feet tall. The lower leaves are numerous, heart shaped, and coarsely toothed. The upper leaves are smaller and tapered at the base. Many flower heads grow on each stem, and the blossoms can be pink, pale blue, violet, or white with a reddish or yellow disk.

HABITAT: common in woods and shady places

BLOOMS: August through October

Asters are sometimes called Christmas daisies (or Michaelmas daisies in England) because they bloom so late in the year. However, most species of asters are less showy than their cousins, the true daisies. The word aster comes from the Latin and Greek words for star. According to Greek legend, the aster was created out of star dust when Virgo, looking down from heaven, wept. Asters were sacred to all the gods and goddesses, and wreaths made from the blossoms were placed on temple altars on festive occasions.

Known in France as "eye of Christ" and in Germany as starworts, asters were often burned to keep away evil spirits. A "mishmash" of asters was thought to cure the bite of a mad dog. The Shakers used the plant to clear their complexions, and the ancient Greeks used it as an antidote for snake bites. The Greeks also thought it helped to drive away snakes. Virgil wrote that boiling aster leaves in wine and placing them close to a hive of bees would improve the honey.

Asters are associated with elegance and daintiness. They were talismans of love and were considered the herb of Venus.

COMMON NAME: **blue-eyed grass**
FAMILY: Iridaceae (Iris)
GENUS: *Sisyrinchium*

DESCRIPTION: The tiny blue flowers with golden stamens are often lost among the grasslike leaves on this plant. There are six sepals, each with a pointed tip. The flowers are light blue, purple, or white on stems that grow as high as twenty inches.

HABITAT: Different species are found in a variety of places, from dry meadows to boggy areas.

BLOOMS: May through July

Because the blue-eyed grasses interbreed easily, identification to the species level is often difficult. This is the smallest member of the Iris family—actually not a grass at all.

The generic name *Sisyrinchium* is from the Greek and is literally translated "pig snout." The reason for this indelicate and seemingly inappropriate name is that wild pigs find the roots delicious and are often seen grubbing for them.

Beautifully contrasting colors are common in nature, and more often than not, there is a reason for these color patterns and combinations. They usually serve to attract pollinators, such as birds and insects, and to point out the way to their own pollen. Entomologists who have studied bees and their ability to see color have found that bees can see four main colors: yellow (and orange), blue, blue-green, and ultraviolet. A color combination of any two of these, such as yellow centers contrasting with a blue blossom as in the blue-eyed grass, is certain to lead the bee to the pollen and insure the flower's pollination.

Blue-eyed grass, planted in a sunny area, can withstand a variety of conditions, and

MCD
© 1983

although the blossoms last only a single day, they open one after another over a long blooming season. This charming little member of the Iris Family transplants easily, even when in bloom, and a few plants will spread into a healthy clump.

COMMON NAME: **bluets**
FAMILY: Rubiaceae (Madder)
GENUS: *Houstonia*
SPECIES: *caerulea*

DESCRIPTION: The flowers of this species have four petals united at the center, which is yellow. The stems grow to heights of only eight inches. The leaves are opposite and are mostly basal, and a single flower grows at the end of the stem. The blossoms are either sky blue or white.

HABITAT: common in grassy places or open woods

BLOOMS: February through April

Common names for this plant include innocence, eyebright (referring to the orange center of the blossom), Venus' pride, little washerwomen, and probably the best known, Quaker ladies. The genus and the species name is Latin for sky blue, descriptive of the color of the petals.

They are pollinated by insects such as the painted lady butterfly and the clouded sulfur butterfly and also by several species of bees.

Bluets adapt well after transplanting and look quite lovely in rock and flower gardens.

Two types of flowers are found in this genus. One has very short stamens and long pistils, and the other is just the opposite, with short pistils and long stamens. They apparently do not interbreed, as only one type is found in a single area.

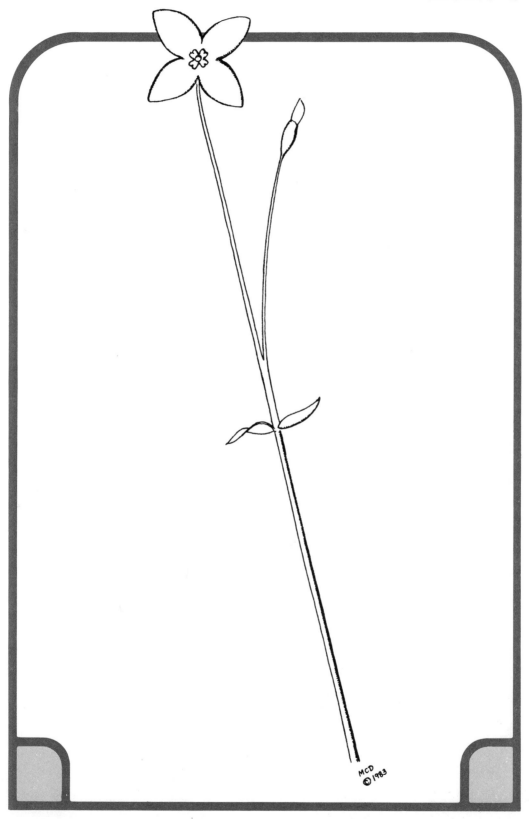

MCD
© 1983

MCD ©1983

COMMON NAME: **burdock**
FAMILY: Compositae (Daisy)
GENUS: *Arctium*
SPECIES: *minus*

DESCRIPTION: The flower head is somewhat thistlelike and is composed of a closely packed cluster of small pinkish purple flowers. The bracts have tiny hooks and form a roundish bur beneath the flower head. The plant is bushy, growing to a height of three to five feet. The lower leaves are long, oblong, and wooly underneath.

HABITAT: roadsides and dry fields

BLOOMS: July through October

Burdock owes its success to the tiny hooks that are found on the bracts below the flower head. Success in the plant world depends on how well the plant is able to spread its seeds and reproduce. The barbed bracts of the burdock stick to animal fur and thus quite efficiently disperse the seed pods over a wide area.

These tiny hooks account for several other common names for this plant, including beggar's buttons, beggar's lice, and hurr burr. The seed pods cling as easily to people as they do to animals and are especially irritating, because they break apart when pulled on, and each piece must be pulled out separately. These tiny hooks were probably the cause for burdock to be used as a symbol for "touch me not."

Original medicinal uses of the plant were based on the doctrine of signatures. (See Introduction.) The seed pods were at one time eaten to help things "stick in your mind." Early pioneers made tea from the roots to help purify the blood and ate the young leaves and roots raw. A brew made from the boiled leaves, honey, and milk was used to treat rheumatism, and a poultice made from boiling the leaves in salt water was said to be good for bruises and swelling.

It was rumored that eating the raw stems of the plant would "stir up lust," and the plant was sometimes used as a love potion. It was also known as love leaves.

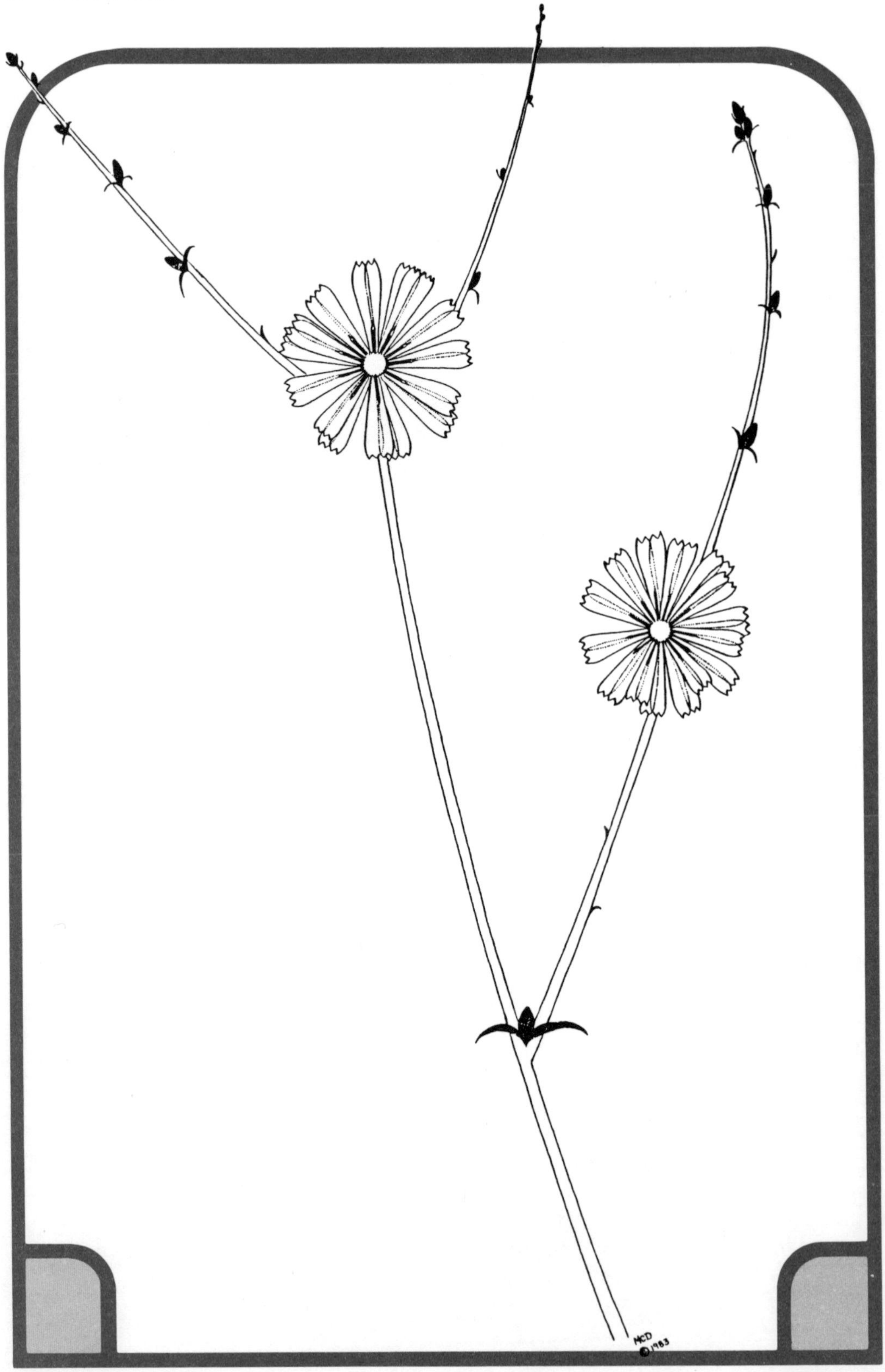
MCD
©1983

COMMON NAME: chicory
FAMILY: Compositae (Daisy)
GENUS: *Cichorium*
SPECIES: *intybus*

DESCRIPTION: A rather ragged looking weed, chicory often grows to a height of four feet. The basal leaves are dark green and deeply toothed, and they taper toward the ends. The upper leaves are much smaller. The tap root is large and grows very deep, and the stem exudes a milky sap when broken open. The flowers are one and a half to two inches across and are a bright blue or azure. Each ray flower extending out from the center is notched or jagged on the ends.

HABITAT: waste places and roadsides; common throughout the eastern United States

BLOOMS: June through October

Probably chicory is best known as a coffee substitute or as an additive in real coffee. It was such a good substitute that often other plants were added to chicory, and then the whole mass was sold as pure chicory. The root was thoroughly cleaned and then roasted until it split. The dark brown centers were ground down and stored in a cool, dry place until used. Chicory coffee is said to be good for liver and gall bladder ailments. The Egyptians and Greeks guzzled chicory coffee and called it the liver's friend. It has been known as a healthful herb for centuries and was mentioned by Pliny and Homer.

A native of Europe, chicory was often cultivated for fodder. When cultivated, the root becomes even larger and very fleshy. Very young leaves were collected and eaten.

The blossoms open in the morning and then face east toward the sun, but will wilt by noon.

Common names include blue sailors, bunk, wild succory, and ragged sailors. The species name *intybus* comes from Latin and means endive. The leaves were often eaten like endive. The name succory comes from the Latin word *succurrere*, "to run under," and refers to the depths to which the roots grow.

The German name for this plant is watcher of the road. A German legend says that a beautiful young girl waited every day for the return of her lover and finally died of a broken heart along the road. The blue chicory grew in the place where she died.

Chicory can be used as a very rough pH indicator, a type of natural litmus paper. For example, children stir up ant hills and then hold the blue flower over the hills. Ants shoot out formic acid as a defense mechanism, and this turns the flower pink.

COMMON NAME: **forget-me-not**
FAMILY: Boraginaceae (Borage)
GENUS: *Myosotis*
SPECIES: *scorpioides*

DESCRIPTION: There are five sky blue petals and a central yellow "eye" on this plant, which grows six to twenty-four inches tall. The flowers occur on curved, diverging branches that uncurl as the blossoms open.

HABITAT: prefers moist areas and streambanks

BLOOMS: May through October

Whispered messages of love, caves full of treasure, and words from God are all found in folklore about the forget-me-not. The name is the same in English, French, and German. A German folktale explains the flower's name: A beautiful blue flower led a man down through the mountains to a cave full of treasures. A lovely lady appeared to the man and said, "forget not the best." The man did not heed her note of warning and took only gold and jewels, leaving the little blue flower behind. As he left the cave carrying his treasures, rocks from the mountains came crashing down, killing the man and closing the cave forever.

Another legend about this little flower tells of a man and his lover who were walking beside a river when the lady saw a beautiful blue flower and asked for it. As the man reached for it, he slipped and fell into the river. He threw the flower to the lady and cried, "forget me not!"

Still another story about the plant's name is that when God was naming all the

plants, the little blue flower with the yellow eye could not remember the name given to it. Finally God whispered to it, "Forget me not, that is your name."

Less charming is the explanation that the leaves are so bitter their taste is never forgotten.

In spite of their bitterness, the leaves were at one time used quite often. Boiled in wine, they were said to be an effective antidote for the bite of an adder, and mixed with oil and wax, they were made into a healing ointment. Egyptians believed if you put the leaves over your eyes during the month of Thoth you would have visions.

Before the plant blooms, the raceme is tightly coiled. To some, this looked like the tail of a scorpion—thus, the species name, *scorpioides*. Based on the doctrine of signatures, the plant was used to treat the stings of spiders and scorpions. The small, rounded leaves gave it another common name, mouse-ear.

If grown in a wildflower garden, forget-me-not needs very moist soil, preferably by a stream. The seeds can be sown anytime.

The forget-me-not is associated with loving remembrance, friendship, and fidelity. It is the state flower of Alaska.

COMMON NAME: **fringed gentian**
FAMILY: Gentianaceae (Gentian)
GENUS: *Gentiana*
SPECIES: *crinita*

DESCRIPTION: The blue, bell-shaped flowers have four petals that are finely dissected at the ends to form the "fringe." The leaves are lanceolate, entire, and opposite. Fringed gentian commonly grows to heights of six to fifteen inches, but can grow as tall as three feet.

HABITAT: very moist woods, stream banks

BLOOMS: August through November

The fringed gentian is considered one of our most beautiful native wildflowers. It blooms very late in the fall, often even after tree leaves have begun to fall. An annual, it grows from seeds dispersed the previous year. Sometimes these seeds get blown great

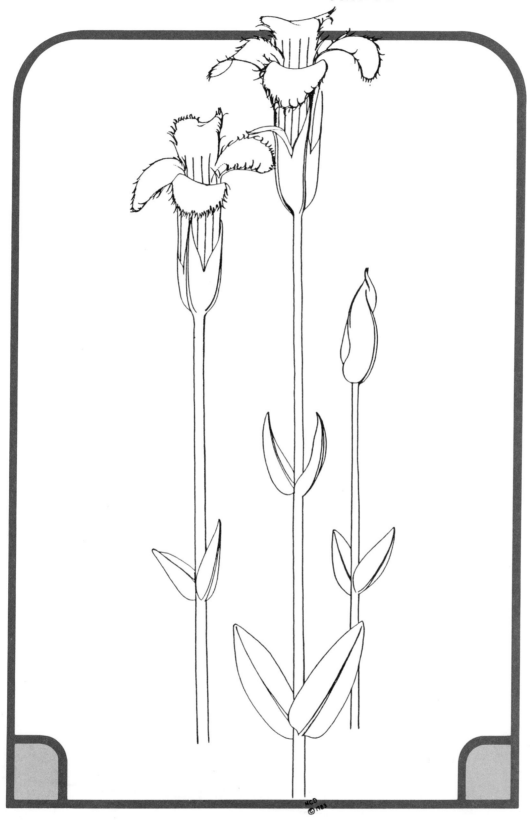

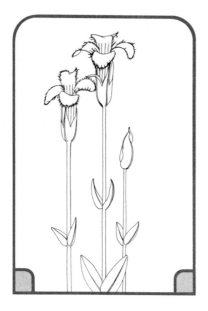

distances from the parent plant, so the plant can turn up in surprising places. Unlike its cousin the closed gentian, the fringed gentian opens during the day and closes up only at night.

One legend says the gentians were named for Gentius, king of Illyria (an ancient country located on the Adriatic Sea). This king was well known for using the gentians for medicine. A Hungarian folk tale says the gentians were named after King Ladislas who, during a terrible plague epidemic, shot an arrow into the air, begging the Lord to let it fall on a plant that he could use to help his people. The arrow landed on a gentian, which was then used with miraculous success to stop the plague.

A concoction called a spring bitter was made from the gentian and used to purify the blood. North American Indians used the plant to ease back pains. Pioneers added a little piece of gentian to gin or brandy to stimulate the appetite and aid in digestion. This was so tasty that there are still several aperitifs that include an extract made from gentian.

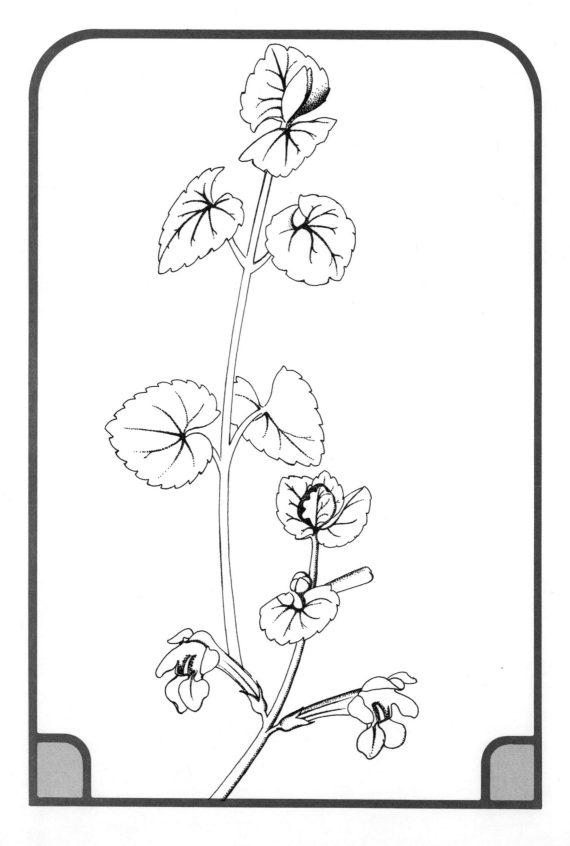

COMMON NAME: **ground ivy**
FAMILY: Labiatae (Mint)
GENUS: *Glechoma*
SPECIES: *hederacea*

DESCRIPTION: This plant is so common in lawns and gardens that it is more often classified as a weed than as a wildflower. It is a ground-hugging plant and has opposite kidney-shaped leaves that have a wrinkled appearance. Like most members of the Labiatae, or Mint Family, this plant is aromatic and has square stems. The scent comes mostly from oil that is found in glands at the base of the downy leaves. The small blossoms are a bluish-purple and occur in the whorls in the leaf axils.

HABITAT: very common in waste places, lawns, and roadsides

BLOOMS: April through July

This plant is abundant almost everywhere, and stories about it have survived from medieval times. It was known as gill-over-the-ground for centuries. The leaves of the plant were added to the vat to clarify and add flavor to beer. Although this method of brewing beer was replaced by hops in the sixteenth century, country folk used gill-over-the-ground for hundreds of years afterward to make their own ale. The word gill comes from the French word *guiller*, "to brew" or "to make merry." The word gill can also mean girl, and this is where another of its names—hedgemaids—comes from. Other common names refer to the shape of the leaf: cat's foot and turn hoof. The common name ground ivy comes from the fact that the leaves are evergreen, like true ivy.

The medicinal uses of the plant are varied. Used as an herbal addition in bath water, it was said to have eased the aging process and to have cured poorly healing wounds. A tea made from the leaves, called gill tea, was an ancient cure for toothaches, gout, deafness, ringing in the ears, and various other aches and pains. Ground ivy leaves were also dried and used as snuff.

Horses will nibble at this plant, but swine and goats will not eat it at all. Farmers must keep a sharp lookout for the plant to keep it out of their pastures, since it is a fierce competitor and will not allow anything else to grow around it. Once started, it is hard to get rid of.

In America, ground ivy was sometimes used as an antidote for lead poisoning from paint.

COMMON NAME: **heal-all**
FAMILY: Labiatae (Mint)
GENUS: *Prunella*
SPECIES: *vulgaris*

DESCRIPTION: A stumpy-looking low plant, *Prunella* grows only six to twelve inches high. The leaves are lance-shaped and measure one to three inches across. The small flowers are bluish lavender and grow on cylindrical-shaped heads close to the stalk. As with other members of the Mint Family, the leaves are opposite and the stems are square.

HABITAT: fields and roadsides throughout Europe, Asia, and North America

BLOOMS: May through October

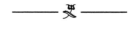

Both the common name and the botanical names refer to the ancient belief in the healing power of the plant. Each blossom has a mouth and throat and so it was once thought to cure diseases of the mouth and throat according to the doctrine of signatures. *Prunella* was originally Brunella from the German word *bruen*, meaning quinsy (an inflammation of the throat). Heal-all is an effective astringent and is useful in stopping the flow of blood from a cut or wound. It has often been used to make a mouth wash by boiling the early spring leaves.

COMMON NAME: hepatica
FAMILY: Ranunculaceae (Buttercup)
GENUS: *Hepatica*
SPECIES: *americana*

DESCRIPTION: Each flower stands on a hairy stem that is four to six inches tall. Five to nine conspicuous sepals are delicate pink, white, or lilac. There are no petals. Under the sepals are three green bracts. The leaves have three lobes and are leathery, often mottled and, in this species, rounded at the tips. New leaves appear after the plant blooms.

HABITAT: prefers shady woodlands

BLOOMS: December through May

Once believed to cure problems of the liver, hepatica is a good example of the doctrine of signatures (see Introduction). Another common name for this plant is round-lobed liverleaf. It was also thought to cure lung diseases. Hepatica is a symbol for confidence and a quick cure.

When farmers saw the small blossoms of hepatica in spring, they knew it would soon be time to start planting.

COMMON NAME: dwarf crested iris
FAMILY: Iridaceae (Iris)
GENUS: *Iris*
SPECIES: *cristata*

DESCRIPTION: The leaves of this plant are grasslike, rising straight up from a scaly rhizome and arching at the tips. The lowest flower parts are the three sepals, which are broad with crinkly edges and purple with an orange band. The next flower parts are the petals, and above them are the narrow stigmas. The height of the plant is only four to nine inches.

HABITAT: rich woods

BLOOMS: April through May

This plant was named by the Greeks for the goddess of the rainbow, Iris, because of the multi-colored flower. Since one of the duties of Iris was to lead the souls of women to the Elysian Fields after they died, Greeks often put iris blossoms on the graves of their women. The name iris is translated as "eye of heaven," a name given both to the center of the eye and to the rainbow.

The iris was prominent in the history of France. As long ago as the first century A.D., the French used the iris to symbolize their victories. Legend tells us that Clovis I, king of the Franks, first adopted the iris as a symbol of victory. His army found itself trapped on one side by an enemy army and a river on the other side. Looking out across the water, Clovis saw a yellow flag iris growing midway across and realized that the river was shallow enough for his army to cross to safety. The iris symbol was revived by Louis VII and was called the flower of Louis, or *fleur-de-lis*. During the reign of Charles IV, the iris was included in the French banner.

Iris was used by American Indians to treat sores on legs. The roots were cleaned and boiled and mashed into a poultice that was applied to the affected area. The root was also commonly used by the Indians as a cathartic. Although it was useful as a medicine, iris does have its hidden poisons. If it is consumed in large quantities, it can cause intestinal inflammation and create a breathing difficulty.

COMMON NAME: **Joe Pye weed**
FAMILY: Compositae (Daisy)
GENUS: *Eupatorium*
SPECIES: *purpureum*

DESCRIPTION: When mature, this impressive plant may grow as tall as six feet. A terminal cluster of many small pinkish purple flowers is slightly fragrant. The leaves occur in whorls of three or four and are toothed. When bruised, the stem gives off a vanilla-like odor.

HABITAT: moist soils, meadows, and low ground

BLOOMS: August through September

Although there are several stories as to who Joe Pye really was, there is a general consensus that he was an Indian medicine man who lived in Colonial New England. He earned his fame by "curing" typhoid fever and several other diseases by using concoctions made from this plant. Another explanation is that the name came from the Indian word for typhoid, *jopi*. Since this plant was supposed to be a cure for the fever, it became known as jopi weed, and later as Joe Pye weed. In the southern Appalachian mountains this plant is called queen-of-the-meadow, a fitting name for this stately herb.

The generic name comes from Mithridates Eupator, a Persian general, who won several important battles against the Romans. He supposedly used this plant as a magical medicine in order to beat the Romans.

The Indians had several uses for the plant. A brave who was courting a young woman was assured of success if he stuck a wad of the plant in his mouth before he went visiting. The Iroquois used it as a remedy for kidney disorders. A hot tea made from the leaves was used to produce sweating to break a fever. Joe Pye weed was also used to improve the appetite and soothe nerves, and if used regularly, the crushed leaves of the plant were said to improve the complexion.

The plant is pollinated by several kinds of insects. Hairs on the flowers hold the pollen and then brush it off on insects that land on the flower. The pollen also brushes off on surrounding flowers, which relieves some of the dependence on insects for pollination.

COMMON NAME: **kudzu**
FAMILY: Leguminosae (Pea)
GENUS: *Pueraria*
SPECIES: *lobata*

DESCRIPTION: This is a very prolific vine, growing to heights of sixty feet or more. The blossom is rather small, pealike, and bluish purple. The compound leaves are large and divided into three rounded lobes.

HABITAT: roadsides, wasteplaces

BLOOMS: July through September

Kudzu's introduction into the United States dates back to 1876 and the Philadelphia Centennial Exposition. In the Japanese Pavilion at this exposition was a "wonder" plant, *Pueraria lobata*, or kudzu. The Japanese used this vine as a forage plant and as food and medicine. They dug and thoroughly cleaned the root and then ground it into a very fine powder, which was a prized food. The leaves, too, were eaten, cooked like other greens. In Japan the plant never became a pest, mainly because of the intensive land-use practices there.

For many years kudzu was thought to be a godsend for eroded areas in the South. Not only did it grow on steep banks of red clay, but it also grew very quickly. It was grown commercially as a forage plant and in areas with poor soil to help enrich the soil.

For a short time it was hailed as "King Kudzu." As kudzu began to "eat" telephone poles and trees, however, people became somewhat disenchanted with this wonder plant. Eventually it was accused of being the plant that ate the South.

Kudzu can grow 80 to 100 feet during a single growing season and will cover just about anything. It is especially noticeable along highways where control measures have not been practiced.

Kudzu is no longer grown commercially, because it is difficult to harvest mechanically and too easy to overgraze. A good grazing goat will do wonders for kudzu control in a short time. Perhaps the highway departments might consider hiring a few goats during the summer months.

Kudzu can be used to make vine

wreaths, though the finished product is not nearly as shiny or graceful as wreaths made with wild grape vines. Today there is little use for the kudzu vine, except to bear the brunt of many a joke.

COMMON NAME: **monkshood**
FAMILY: Ranunculaceae (Buttercup)
GENUS: *Aconitum*
SPECIES: *uncinatum*

DESCRIPTION: Monkshood blossoms are violet colored and are irregularly shaped, looking almost hooded. There are five large purple sepals and four to six very small petals. Several blossoms are generally grouped at the top of the flowering stem. The toothed leaves are palmately divided and are alternate. The plant stands from two to four feet tall.

HABITAT: open woods, moist hillsides

BLOOMS: August through October

This plant is so poisonous it has been called the "queen mother of poisons." Poisoning from the plant causes first a tingling sensation and then numbness. The juice was used to poison Greek and Roman arrows and the bait left for wolves. The latter use gained it the name wolf's bane. Although the root is the most poisonous part, all parts of the plant are poisonous, especially immediately before blooming.

As with many poisonous plants, a little bit—handled correctly—can be quite beneficial. A drug, Aconite, is derived from monkshood and is used as a heart and nerve sedative.

Because the sepals are curved and resemble helmets or hoods, the plant lends itself to a variety of common names. The name monkshood comes from the resemblance of these sepals to the hats or hoods worn by medieval monks. Others thought they looked like the kind of hat monkeys wear in the circus and called it monkey's cap or monk's cap.

The generic name, *Aconitum*, is from the hill Aconitus, on which Hercules was thought to have fought with Cerberus, the multi-headed watchdog of the underworld. The legend says the foam from Cerberus' mouth was flung across the countryside as the great dog shook his head. Where this foam landed, the poisonous monkshood was thought to have grown.

Although monkshood does reproduce easily, it is not recommended for cultivation because it is so poisonous. Surprisingly, despite its poisonous properties, the language of monkshood is chivalry and knight-errantry.

COMMON NAME: **wild onion**
FAMILY: Liliaceae (Lily)
GENUS: *Allium*
SPECIES: *stellatum*

DESCRIPTION: Wild onion leaves are grasslike and grow close together from a bulb. They are six to eight inches tall, but are slightly shorter than the flowering stem. The flowers are lavender. The leaves wilt at the time of flowering. The broken stem exudes a very strong onion odor.

HABITAT: prefers grassy open spaces

BLOOMS: July through September

Since the onion has an unfavorable reputation because of its pungent smell, most people are surprised to find what a lovely blossom it has. These dainty lavender petals give the plant an entirely different personality when it is in bloom.

Dairymen dread seeing onions growing in their fields, because if cows get into a patch of wild onion their milk tastes sour. Both the bulb and leaves smell and taste like onion. The bulb was used on the Lewis and Clark expedition to flavor the explorers' dull camp food.

The Winnebago and Dakota Indian tribes used the onion for treating bee and wasp stings. The eastern Indians would slice an onion, wrap it in cloth, and tie it around their wrists when they were ill. They believed it drew out fever from the body, and when the onion turned brown, all the fever would be gone. According to another superstition about onions, if you wore one around your neck, it would prevent diseases from entering your body. Onions also were said to alleviate dizzy spells and cure gall bladder problems. Boiled and made into a tea, it was considered a good treatment for croup in children. Made into a poultice, it would bring boils to a head.

Bears and ground squirrels eat wild onion roots, and elk and deer eat the leaves.

COMMON NAME: **passionflower**
FAMILY: Passifloraceae (Passionflower)
GENUS: *Passiflora*
SPECIES: *incarnata*

DESCRIPTION: This is a very easy plant to identify, because it is distinguished by a purple-fringed crown. There are five sepals, five petals, five stamens, and three styles in its one to two-inch wide flowers. The three leaves are deeply lobed. The fruit is fleshy and yellow. This fairly common vine may creep ten feet or more.

HABITAT: common in fields, roadsides, and thin woods

BLOOMS: May through August

Named *flos passionis* or *flor de las cinco llagas* (flower of the five wounds) by the Jesuits, passion flower is believed to be the flower that grew on the cross in a vision seen by St. Francis of Assissi. Each part of the flower is believed to be representative of the instruments of the Passion. The five sepals and the five petals taken together represent the ten faithful apostles (Peter, having denied the Lord, and Judas, having betrayed Him, were not included). The fringed crown, of course, represents the crown of thorns, and the five stamens represent the five wounds. The ovary represents the hammer, and the three styles the nails.

The common name May-pop is from the fruit, which forms in late summer. It is yellowish and is edible. Some Indian tribes believed that the May-pop fruit would cure insomnia and soothe nerves. When the Jesuits found the Indians eating the fruit they took it as a sign that the Indians were hungry for Christianity and began, with great zeal, to convert them, managing to succeed in a short time. The species name means flesh colored.

Passionflower is considered a symbol of faith and piety. It is the state flower of Tennessee.

COMMON NAME: **spiderwort**
FAMILY: Commelinaceae (Spiderwort)
GENUS: *Tradescantia*
SPECIES: *virginiana*

DESCRIPTION: The three roundish petals of one-to-two-inch flowers are purplish blue and are all the same size. There are six rather conspicuous stamens and a hairy stem. Two to four grasslike leaves may be a foot long.

HABITAT: common in pastures and moist woods

BLOOMS: April through July

The generic name comes from a father-son botany team, the John Tradescants. John T., Sr. was royal gardener to the English king, Charles I, and was responsible for bringing several unusual plants into England, including the gladiolus and the apricot. John, Jr. did his share of collecting, and it was he who first brought the spiderwort to England from Virginia.

There are two possible origins for the common name for the spiderwort. The more commonly accepted one is that the leaves, which are somewhat twisted at the joints, resemble the spreading legs of spiders. Alice M. Coats, suggests another in her book *Flowers and Their Histories*: the spiderwort was once classified as one of the "phlangiums," which supposedly would cure the bite of the phlangium spider. She explains that there is

really nothing magical about that cure, as the phlangiums are harmless anyway.

Due to the action of certain enzymes within the plant, the dead blossoms do not shrivel and fall off as most other blossoms do, but instead turn into a runny blob. This characteristic gave the plant other common names, widow's tears and the Moses-in-the-bulrushes. Another common name is the Trinity flower, inspired by the three petals.

Spiderwort is of special interest to research botanists, because it is a historic link between the sedges and the lilies, and also because the chromosomes are very large (relatively speaking) and are often used for the study of cytology.

Recent research has created much interest in this plant. It was found that spiderwort is particularly sensitive to pollution and radiation and will undergo mutations that cause the blossoms to change from blue to pink within two weeks of being exposed to severe levels of pollution. The number of cells that mutate directly correlates with the severity of the dose of pollution. Thus the spiderwort has become a cheap detection device and has encouraged researchers to look for other plants that might be used in the same way.

COMMON NAME: **spotted knapweed**
FAMILY: Compositae (Daisy)
GENUS: *Centaurea*
SPECIES: *maculosa*

DESCRIPTION: The flowers of this plant look somewhat like those of the thistle; they are lavender blue and are composed entirely of disk flowers. The bracts below the flower heads are prickly and have black tips. The stem is branching and grows to a height of two to three feet.

HABITAT: dry fields, waste places

BLOOMS: June through August

Most of the common names for this plant refer to the flower bud, which is round and hard and looks like a button sitting on top of thistlelike bracts. The bracts are responsible for one of its common names, star thistle. The name knapweed is from the German word *knobbe*, which means a bump or button. Other common names are hardhead and blue bottle. It was also known as bachelor's button, since the bud resembled a kind of button (like a cuff link) that required no sewing and was thought useful for bachelors. At one time English girls wore these bachelor button flowers as a sign that they were eligible to marry. It was also thought that if a girl hid this flower under her apron she could have the bachelor of her choice. The name corn flower was given to this plant because it was often found growing in grain fields. (In England corn was not the American maize, but was considered any sort of grain growing.)

The species name means spotted and refers to the black tipped bracts. The origin of the generic name is more complicated. At

MCD
© 1984

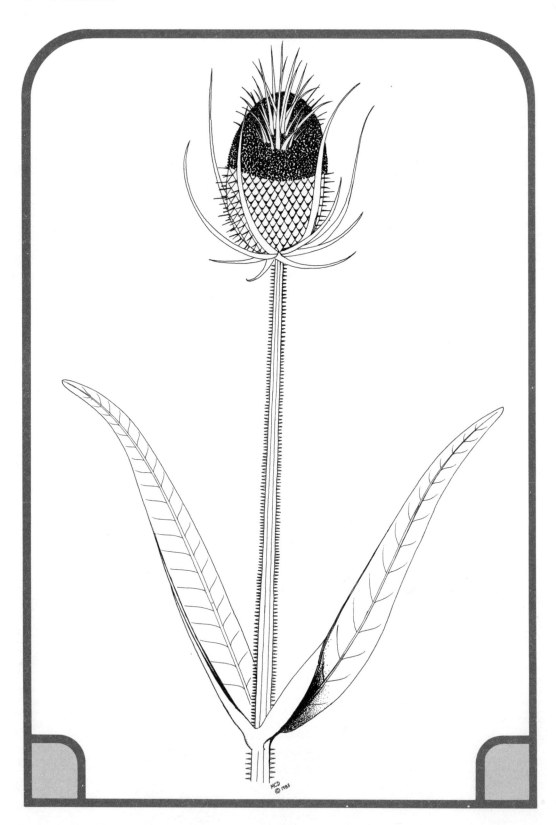

one time the gentian flowers were called centaurium because they helped to heal Chiron, who was a centaur accidentally wounded by Hercules's poisonous arrows. In 288 B.C. a Greek philosopher tried to identify knapweed and called it a gentian, or a centaurium, by mistake. For some reason the name stuck and is still with us today.

Although North Africans were reported to have fed the plant to their camels, consumption of knapweed has been minimal.

More than 600 varieties of knapweed are found mostly in Europe and Eastern Asia.

COMMON NAME: **teasel**
FAMILY: Dipsacaceae (Teasel)
GENUS: *Dipsacus*
SPECIES: *sylvestris*

DESCRIPTION: The flower head is egg shaped and covered with spines that nearly cover up the small lavender flowers. The flowers begin to bloom in a band around the center of the flower head. New ones open up above and below the band. The bracts under the flower head are long, prickly, and curved upward. The stem is also covered with small spines. The leaves are long, toothed, and opposite. The plant grows to two to six feet.

HABITAT: old fields and roadsides

BLOOMS: July through October

The teasel was brought from Europe by wool manufacturers because the dried seed head, fastened to a spindle, was used extensively to "tease" or comb the nap of woolen cloth—thus, the name. It was also called gypsy comb.

In some species, the leaves clasp the stem, and when it rains, water collects in pools at the base of the leaves. This water was thought to be very special and was much sought after. For instance, it was thought to be an especially good thirst-quencher for the traveler. The genus name reflects this property of the plant; it is based on the Greek word for thirst, *dipsa*. This special water was also used to bathe tired eyes and remove warts. It supposedly could make you as beautiful as Venus, and the plant is also called Venus' basin. The species name means growing in the woods.

The flower heads keep their shape throughout the winter and are very good to use in dried flower arrangements.

COMMON NAME: **thistle**
FAMILY: Compositae (Daisy)
GENUS: *Cirsium*
SPECIES: *vulgare*

DESCRIPTION: The thistle is easily recognized by the prickly "wings" that protect the flower from predators and wildflower pickers. The stem is stout and branching, rising to a height of about three to six feet. The basal leaves are deeply segmented. The purple flower heads are nine to twelve inches across.

HABITAT: found in fields, woods and roadsides

BLOOMS: June through October

Although the stickers on the branches of the thistle may discourage people from picking the flower, not all animals are in such awe of the plant. Goldfinches feed off the fluffy seeds, and the caterpillar of the thistle butterfly spins its web around the leaves. At least one other organism shares our dislike of the dense wooly hairs on the stem, however. These hairs block ants from reaching the nectar in the flowers.

This plant is often called bull thistle, perhaps because it frequently grows in pastures where cattle graze.

Thistle is the national emblem of the Scots. The use of thistle dates back to the time when the Danes invaded Scotland. Legend says that the Danes, hoping to sneak up on the Scots, took off their boots and were creeping through the fields when one soldier stepped on a prickly thistle and cried out. The Scots were warned and were able to defend themselves and their country. From this legend came the superstition that whoever wore the thistle was safe from harm.

Since the language of this plant is

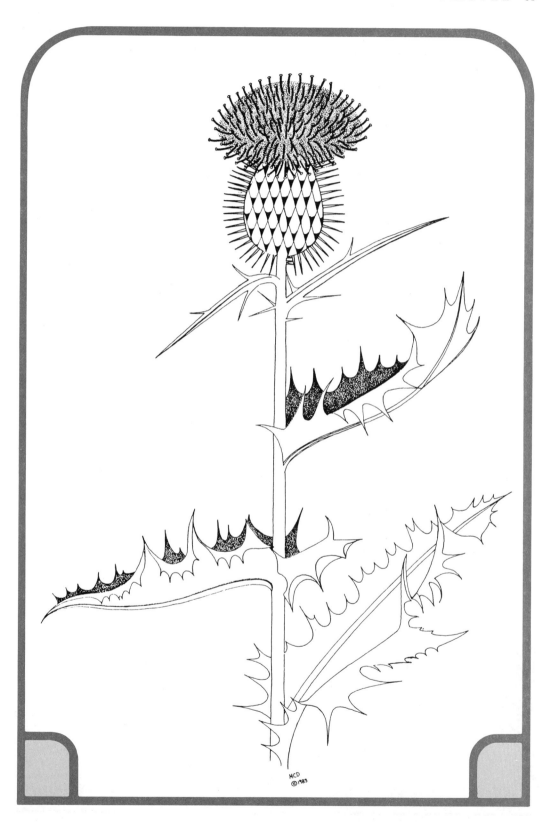

MCD
©1983

defiance and surliness, a young lady would probably not be pleased to see thistle in her bouquet from an admirer.

Dedicated to Thor, god of thunder, thistle is often called the lightning plant.

COMMON NAME: **vetch**
FAMILY: Leguminosae (Pea)
GENUS: *Vicia*
SPECIES: *dasycarpa*

DESCRIPTION: The leaves are pinnately divided into six to eight pairs and are characterized by tendrils or hairlike extensions at the end of the leaves. These tendrils allow this vine to trail and climb. The flowers are purple with white wings on each side.

HABITAT: roads, wasteplaces, and pastures

BLOOMS: April through September

Although this is a native of Europe, it now grows throughout North America. It was first imported as a forage plant, so it can be correctly termed an "escape plant," a plant that was once cultivated, but has adapted to grow quite well in the wild. Like many other plants, this species can help the woodsman determine what kind of weather a particular area experienced. If vetch blooms in March, then the preceeding winter was mild. If the winter was a harsh one, then the vetch will not bloom until later.

Vetch is used for fodder, as a ground cover, and for soil improvement. It is often sown in orchards to improve the quality of the soil. A certain type of bacteria grows on the roots of the vetch and most other members of the pea family. This bacteria can change free nitrogen into a usable form and actually put nitrogen into the soil.

The names vetch and *Vicia* come from the Latin word *vincire*, "to twist or bind," and is descriptive of the growing habits of the plant.

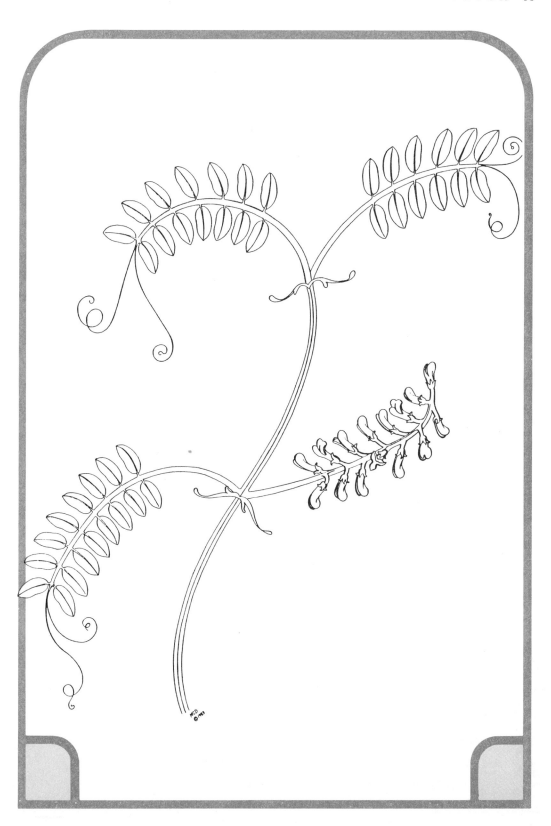

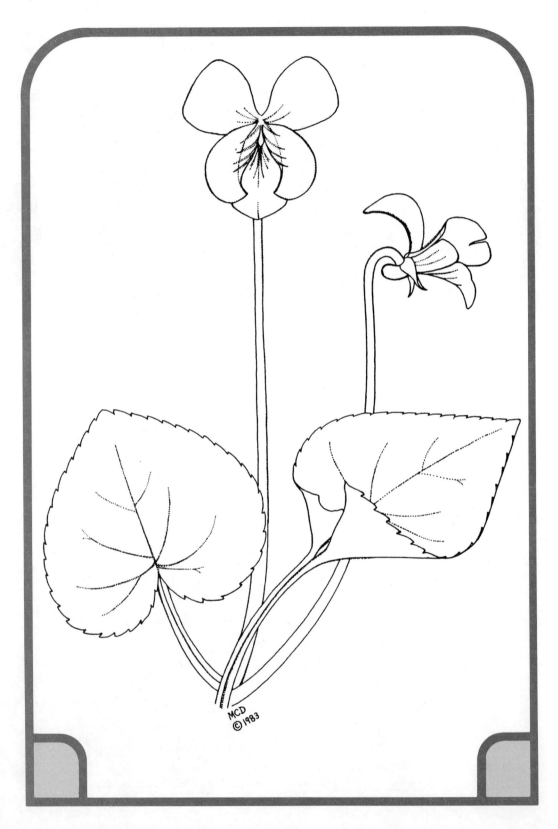

COMMON NAME: **violet**
FAMILY: Violaceae
GENUS: *Viola*

DESCRIPTION: Most of the violets found in the United States are in the genus *Viola*. These are characterized by a lower petal with a hollow spur and a wide landing pad for insects. Although it is easy to tell whether or not you have a violet, it is sometimes difficult to determine which species of violet you have. Violets most often have five petals and five sepals.

HABITAT: Violets grow in several kinds of areas, though as a rule they prefer shady woods.

BLOOMS: spring and summer

The violet is and always has been a very favorite wildflower. There are about eighty species of violets in the United States. It is the state flower of Illinois, New Jersey, Rhode Island, and Wisconsin.

Perhaps no other wildflower mythology is as well known as that of the violet. Legend holds that the nymph Io was loved by Zeus. To hide her from his jealous wife, Hera, Zeus changed Io into a white heifer. Io was not used to the rough grass she was forced to eat and began to cry. Zeus, taking pity on her, changed her tears into sweet smelling flowers which were later called violets. The Greek word Io means Violet. Another version of the story says that Hera, angry at finding Io with Zeus, was the one who turned Io into a heifer. Still another version says the violets were created for Io to honor her beauty.

Much later in history, during the exile of their leader, the French Bonapartists chose the violet as their symbol, since Napoleon had promised to return with the violets in the spring. He kept his promise and returned to Paris on March 20, 1815.

The violet is a symbol of modesty and simplicity, and is considered the herb of Zeus. Shakespeare was very fond of the violet and included it often in his love sonnets. He used the flower as a symbol of humility and constancy in love.

The medicinal and culinary virtues of violets were discovered before Rome was an empire. In those times the women would mix

violets in goat's milk and apply it to their faces to help their complexions. Pliny recommended violets to induce sleep, strengthen the heart muscles, and calm anger. Wearing a garland of violets was said to dispel the odors of wine and spirits and thus prevent drunkenness.

Modern times find us still using the violet. The leaves are high in vitamins A and C and can be eaten raw in salads or cooked like greens. Violets have been called wild okra, because the leaves get stringy when cooked, just as okra does. They were often used in soups and sauces as thickening agents. The flowers can be made into candy, jam, jelly, or syrup and have been used to make a passable wine. Made into a tea, violets will help get rid of a headache. Made into a poultice, the plant is useful in curing ulcers and bedsores. To smell violets was thought to cause a temporary loss of smell.

Before more sophisticated methods were developed, chemists often used the juice from crushed violet blossoms to determine how much acid or base was contained in a substance. When touched by an acid the juice turns red, and if touched by a base, it turns green.

Although the plants will survive a wide range of soil conditions, the number of flowers they produce is dependent on the type of soil they are grown in. The better the soil conditions, the more blossoms will be produced. This can be used as a very rough indication of how rich the soil is in a particular area.

Many violets produce two types of flowers. Spring blossoms are large and showy to attract insects. Since most species of violets have a wide lower petal for insects to land on, pollination occurs easily. Summer flowers are "blind" flowers. They never open, have no petals, and grow close to the ground. These are self-pollinated and insure the seed production for the next growing season in case the spring flowers were not pollinated due to cold or rainy weather.

Some of the more common types of violets include:

Birdfoot violet (*Viola pedata*). This one is easy to identify because of the deeply segmented leaves, which resemble the claws of a crow. The flowers are large, often measuring one and a half inches across. The stems grow to a height of four to ten inches. Usually the five petals are all lilac colored, but sometimes the two lower petals are a darker color. The stamens are an orange or yellow color. This violet prefers a dry, open, sandy area or open woods. It blooms from March to fall.

Common blue violet (*Viola papilionacea*). This is the most common violet. The petals are all lilac colored or sometimes white toward the center. The stems are smooth and are no taller (three to eight inches) than the stems that bear the leaves. The leaves are heart shaped and by mid-summer are sometimes as large as five inches across. The preferred habitat is dry meadows, open roadsides, or woods. It blooms from late February to June. The Confederate violet, a color variation of the common blue violet, is white with purple veins. It is called the Confederate violet, because it is so commonly seen growing around the doorways of Southern homes.

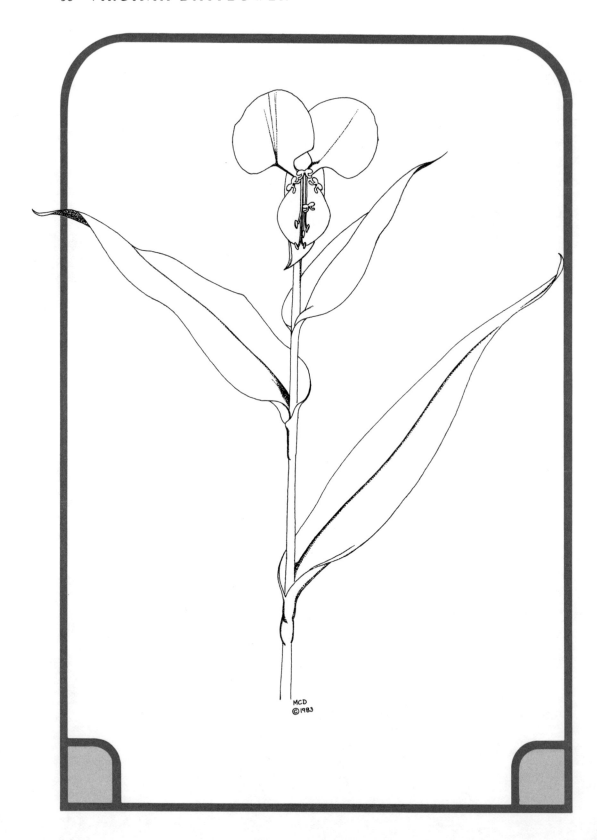

COMMON NAME: **Virginia dayflower**
FAMILY: Commelinaceae (Spiderwort)
GENUS: *Commelina*
SPECIES: *virginica*

DESCRIPTION: The grasslike leaves of this plant often make it difficult to find when it grows among weeds and grass. The plant grows to a height of one and a half to three feet. The blossoms are rather small, with three petals. The upper two petals are much larger than the lower one, but the lower one supports the stamens. All the petals are a bluish purple. A similar species, the Asiatic dayflower, has two blue petals and one white one.

HABITAT: common in woods and clearings

BLOOMS: July through October

Both the family and genus names for this plant are based on a Dutch family name, Commelin. Two of the Commelin brothers were very active in the field of botany and contributed many scholarly papers. The third brother died quite young without publishing any botanical works of his own. Linnaeus found a similarity in the dayflower, which has two large petals and one small one, and the three brothers, two well known and one little known.

The common name comes from the fact that the blossoms last only a single day.

The roots, boiled and served with white sauce, make a tasty substitute for creamed potatoes. The young leaves were eaten in salads. Superstition held that the raw leaves would increase sexual potency, especially among the older folks. It was also fed to stud animals before breeding.

COMMON NAME: **wild lupine**
FAMILY: Leguminosae (Pea)
GENUS: *Lupinus*
SPECIES: *perennis*

DESCRIPTION: The blue, pealike flowers of the wild lupine grow on a tall raceme. The lower leaves are palmately divided into seven to eleven leaflets. The plant grows to a height of eight to twenty-four inches.

HABITAT: sandy soils, dry clearings

BLOOMS: April through July

Of the many species in this genus, probably the best known is *L. texensis*, the Texas bluebonnet. Several hybrid crossings of the genus are now cultivated.

Lupinus comes from the Latin *lupus* meaning wolf. It was thought that the lupine robbed the soil of its richness, just as wolves robbed the shepherds. Actually, as a member of the Leguminosae Family, lupine puts nitrogen into the soil, leaving it richer than before. Lupine can thrive in dry, poor soil.

Other common names for this plant include old maid's bonnets and sundial plant. The leaves follow the sun's path from morning until dusk, finally folding completely together at night. This reduction in the surface area of the leaves prevents unnecessary chilling from the night air.

The lupine, according to a thirteenth-century herbal, was useful in healing the spot left after an infant's umbilical cord was cut.

The flower is easy to cultivate and does well in a wildflower garden. Because its deep taproot is difficult to transplant, young seedlings are usually more satisfactory for starting a stand than transplanting older plants.

The language of lupine is voraciousness and imagination.

MCD
© 1983

COMMON NAME: **wood sorrel**
FAMILY: Oxalidaceae (Wood Sorrel)
GENUS: *Oxalis*
SPECIES: *violacea*

DESCRIPTION: This plant is very similar to the yellow wood sorrel (*Oxalis stricta*). The violet wood sorrel has three cloverlike leaflets that are deep purple underneath. The blossoms have five violet-colored petals.

HABITAT: Not as common as the sister plant, *Oxalis stricta*, the wood sorrel is found occasionally in rich woods and rocky places.

BLOOMS: April through May

Another name for the wood sorrel is wild shamrock. Nearly everyone recognizes the shamrock as the St. Patrick's Day flower. The association stems from an Irish legend: When St. Patrick was a missionary, trying to explain the Doctrine of the Trinity, he had trouble getting the idea across. The chief of a tribe asked how one could be three. St. Patrick, seeing a shamrock growing close by, bent and picked a leaf and said, "Here in this leaf, three in one, this is a symbol of my faith, Three Gods in One." The chief was impressed by the analogy and professed his faith.

Even before the time of St. Patrick, the wood sorrel or wild shamrock was a mystic emblem for Druids in Ireland and was associated with the Celtic sun wheel.

Wood sorrel is a symbol for joy and maternal tenderness.

BROWN & GREEN FLOWERS

❁

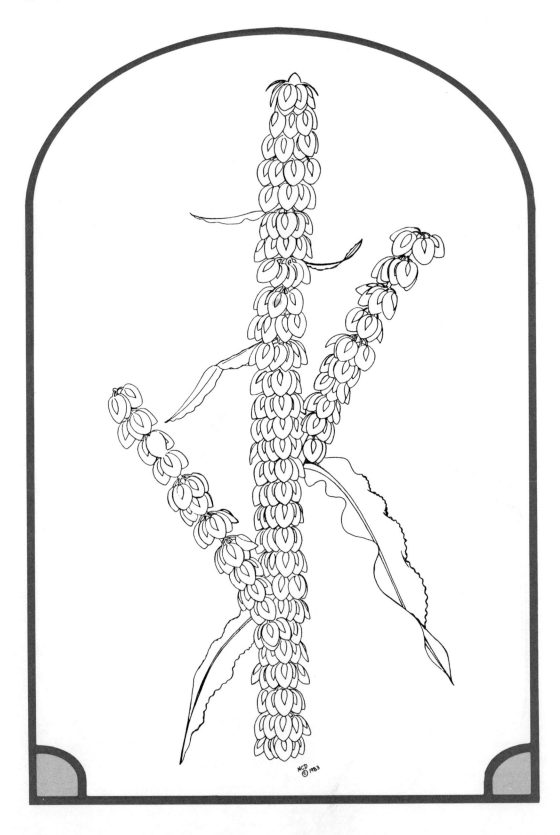

COMMON NAME: **curly dock**
FAMILY: Polygonaceae (Buckwheat)
GENUS: *Rumex*
SPECIES: *crispus*

DESCRIPTION: This plant grows two to four feet tall. The leaves are dark green and are characterized by wavy edges. The flowers are also green and are found on a dense spike. The seeds turn a rust color and are especially noticeable in the fall.

HABITAT: very common in waste places and roadsides

BLOOMS: June through September

One of the best-known uses of curly dock is as dried material in arrangements or in natural Christmas wreaths.

Dock is a health food enthusiast's ambrosia. It has more vitamin C than orange juice and more vitamin A than carrots. Both the leaves and the seeds are edible and have a lemonish taste. George Washington Carver is said to have used dock as a substitute for rhubarb in rhubarb pie. It has been used as a tonic since 500 B.C. and is listed in several old herbals as being good for "loose teeth." Since scurvy was a common disease that affected teeth and gums, and since vitamin C is a cure for scurvy, dock could very well have helped to "tighten up" teeth.

Dock is related to domestic buckwheat. The seeds were used by American Indians in the West in flour and meal. The root was used as a laxative and a tonic. If the root is boiled with meat, it is said to make the meat cook faster.

The name dock is Latin and was the name for the solid part of an animal's tail. The expression "to dock" meant to remove the animal's tail, usually in reference to sheep or dogs. The species name is also from the Latin and means curly.

According to the doctrine of signatures (see Introduction), the yellow root of the dock was used to treat jaundice.

The language of dock is patience.

COMMON NAME: **heart leaf**
FAMILY: Aristolochiaceae (Birthwort)
GENUS: *Hexastylis*
SPECIES: *arifolia*

DESCRIPTION: The most conspicuous feature of this plant is the hairy leaves that grow quite close to the ground, usually no more than four to five inches tall. The flowers are quite small and sometimes hard to find; they, too, grow close to the ground. They are purplish brown, have no petals, and are shaped like a bell with three lobes.

HABITAT: common in rich, shady, moist woods

BLOOMS: April through May

Heart leaf is often called wild ginger, because of the gingerlike odor in the roots. It is sometimes used as ginget flavoring. In the southern Appalachian mountains, candied ginger is made by cutting the root, boiling it until tender and then dipping it in a heavy syrup. The word ginger comes from the Sanskrit word *srngaverem*, which means "horn body" and also refers to the shape of the blossoms. The blossoms are called little brown jug or little pig's feet.

Heart leaf has always been associated with childbirth; the common name for the family is Birthwort. Mountain women often used the root to ease the aches and pains of pregnancy. American Indians used it as a contraceptive (with questionable success) by boiling the root in hot water and drinking it as a tea. This type of tea was also often used to treat whooping cough and a variety of other ills. Modern research has found that the plant contains chemicals that are effective antibiotics.

Not bright and showy enough to attract butterflies or bees, this plant is pollinated by a beetle that crawls deep inside the flower.

In a yard with deep shade and fairly rich soil, heart leaf makes a lovely ground cover. With sufficient moisture the plant can survive with very little sun.

COMMON NAME: Jack-in-the-pulpit
FAMILY: Araceae (Arum)
GENUS: *Arisaema*
SPECIES: *triphyllum*

DESCRIPTION: These flowers are unisexual, with the male parts on the top of the plants and the female parts below. The flower is easily identified by the hood that arches over the rest of the plant. The upper part is green or purplish brown and often striped. One to two leaves are usually palmately divided into three to five leaflets. The berries are bright red and can be found in clusters in the fall. The height of the plant is one to three feet.

HABITAT: common in rich, moist woods

BLOOMS: March through June

This plant has an especially descriptive name. The pulpit is the arching spathe, while the Jack is the green spadix in the lower part of the plant.

When city boys came to visit the country, the more knowledgeable country boys would introduce them to the country by giving them a bite of the Jack-in-the-pulpit. At first the plant would taste fine but after a while a burning sensation would begin and would cause an inflammation of the throat and mouth that lasted for hours. Calcium oxalate crystals in the plant become imbedded in the tissues of the mouth and provoke a burning sensation. Cold milk alleviates the condition slightly. This is a plant that should not be touched and certainly not eaten unless prepared correctly. The root must be dried and boiled before it is eaten. American Indians used the powdered root in making flour. The root was also often pounded into a pulp and then applied to the forehead in an attempt to cure headaches. This plant was also called Indian turnip.

The leaves and the red fruit are eaten by ring-necked pheasants and wild turkey.

The language of the Jack-in-the-pulpit is ardor and zeal.

COMMON NAME: **milkweed**
FAMILY: Asclepiadaceae (Milkweed)
GENUS: *Asclepias*
SPECIES: *syriaca*

DESCRIPTION: As well known for its oblong-shaped seed pods as for its umbel of lavender or green flowers, milkweed often grows to heights of two to six feet. The stems are somewhat stout, and the leaves are paired, oblong, or oval and are rounded at the ends and quite pointed at the tips. During the fall when the seed pods are conspicuous, the pods burst open all of a sudden, shooting forth hundreds of silken parachute seeds. These pods are covered with woolly bumps called warts.

HABITAT: common along dry roadsides in thickets and fields

BLOOMS: June through August

Pee-too-can-oh-uk is the Delaware name for milkweed boiled with dumplings. If the sap is removed and the plant is carefully prepared, all parts of the young plant are edible. The young sprouts can be cooked and eaten like asparagus.

The generic name comes from the Greek god of medicine, whose Latin name is Aesculapius. Although today no medicinal value is attributed to the plant, at one time the root was used extensively as a healing herb. The Quebec Indians used the roots as a contraceptive, and the Shawnee Indians used the white sap to take away warts. The root was chewed for dysentery, and the dried leaves were mixed with tobacco and smoked in a pipe to help asthma.

The common name comes from the milky juice in the stems. During World War II researchers tried to make rubber from the sap. The expense and trouble of extracting the sap from the plant in relation to the amount of rubberlike material gained made the process impractical. This milky juice in the stem protects the plant from ants: their feet puncture the stem and get caught up in the sticky white stuff.

All of the 1,900 species of the milkweed

depend on insects for pollinization. Because they depend so heavily on insects, some fairly sophisticated mechanisms developed to insure that the insects do the job. When an insect lands on a petal, it must scramble for a footing because the surface of the petal is slippery. In the scramble, the feet get caught in the base of the flower. In its struggles to get out, the insect is thoroughly doused with pollen, which it obligingly takes along to the next blossom.

The milkweed seeds are on long silky parachutes that the wind carries for great distances. Goldfinches use these parachutes to line their nests. Some of the tougher parts of the plant, such as the fiber, can be used to make string or cord.

The monarch butterfly is often called the milkweed butterfly because the larvae feed on milkweed plants. Other insects that feed on the milkweed include bees, wasps, flies, and beetles.

COMMON NAME: **stinging nettle**
FAMILY: Urticaceae (Nettle)
GENUS: *Urtica*
SPECIES: *dioica*

DESCRIPTION: This entire plant is covered with coarse, stinging hairs or bristles. Several thin branches of tiny green flowers occur in the leaf axils. Male and female flowers are often found on separate plants. The leaves are heart shaped and opposite. Stinging nettle will grow to a height of two to four feet.

HABITAT: wasteplaces, roadsides

BLOOMS: June through September

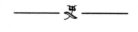

The hairs that give this plant its name are hollow, but are connected to cells containing ammonia and formic acid. Relief from the sting comes from rubbing leaves of dock, rhubarb, rosemary, mint, or sage over the irritated skin. It is interesting to note that stinging nettle and dock are nearly always found growing close together, almost as if by design.

It was thought that apples that grew over nettle plants were bigger and ripened more quickly. Since nettle plants indicate soil rich

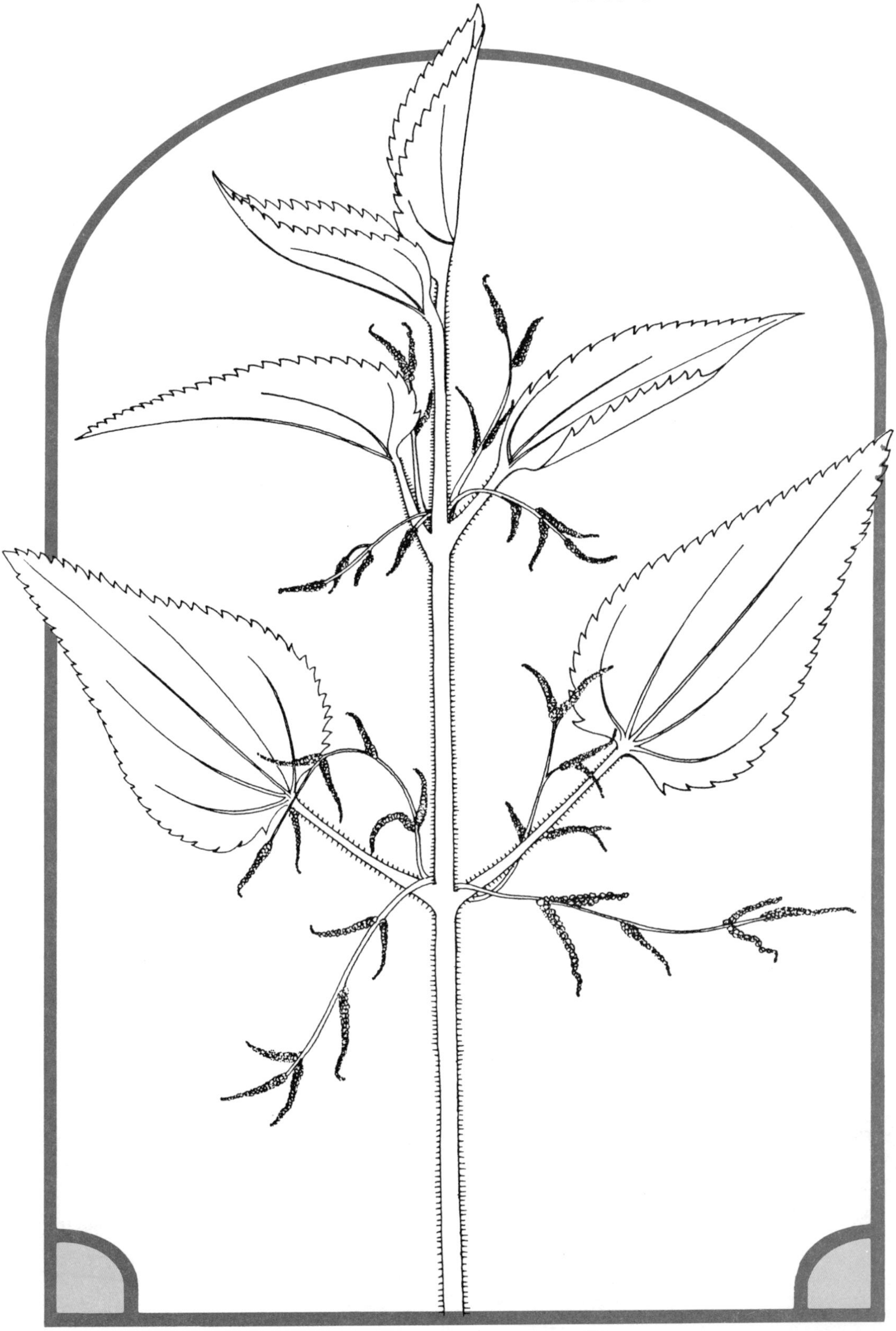

in nitrogen, there may be some substance in the belief.

The genus name, *Urtica*, refers to the stinging properties of the plant. It is from the Latin word, *uro*, which means "I burn." The species name is from the Greek word meaning "two households"; the plant was so named because male and female flowers occur on different plants. The word nettle is derived from net or net plant, which it was called because fibers from the plant were used as twine or woven into cloth.

According to the doctrine of signatures, the profusion of hairs on the plant indicate that eating the plant would stimulate hair growth. A concoction made from the plant was used on burns, and cloth soaked in nettle juice was reputed to be good for a nosebleed.

Nettle leaves were boiled and eaten like other greens. Parts of the plant were even used to make beer.

Nettle is also useful to the gardener. If added to a compost pile, it is said to speed the decaying process. A natural pesticide can be made by boiling the roots and leaves in water for half an hour, then straining the liquid off and spraying for aphids and flea beetles.

COMMON NAME: skunk cabbage
FAMILY: Araceae (Arum)
GENUS: *Symplocarpus*
SPECIES: *foetidus*

DESCRIPTION: The flowers of this plant are quite small and inconspicuous. They are borne on a knoblike spadix, which is hidden within a mottled green and dark purple hoodlike spathe. The leaves appear in late spring and look like cabbage leaves.

HABITAT: swamps and marshes

BLOOMS: February through May

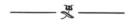

This "hermit of the bog" is unfortunately best known for its particularly offensive smell. This smell accounts for its common name and also for the species name, *foetidus*, which means "evil smelling." The genus name is from two Greek words, *symploke* and *karpos*, which mean "connected fruit." This refers to the fruiting stalk, which is the result of the ovaries growing together. Other common names are clumpfoot cabbage and polecat weed.

The saving grace of the skunk cabbage is that it blooms so early in the spring, seeming to defy winter and cold and death as the

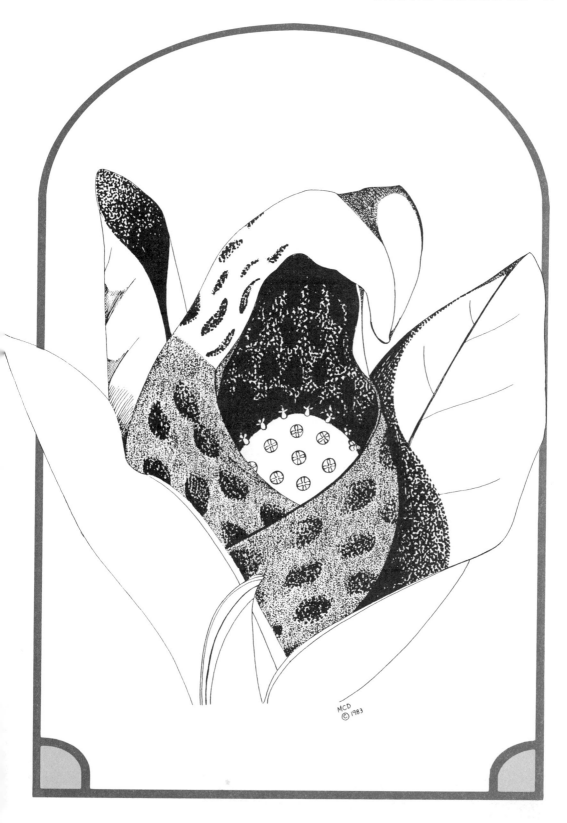

MCD
© 1983

new shoots shove the old withered leaves out of the way. The tightly coiled green spathe will even come through snow in February. After the plant is pollinated, the leaves uncurl and grow to two feet or more. The reddish color of the plant resembles meat and helps to attract carrion flies, as does the wretched odor. As the plant grows it produces heat. Temperatures within the buds of the plant have been recorded to be 27 degrees F. warmer than the temperature of the outside air. This heat not only helps protect the bud from very cold weather, but also intensifies the odor and thus helps to draw more pollinators.

Skunk cabbage was at one time much sought after as a contraceptive. It was thought that one tablespoon three times a day for three weeks would cause permanent sterility in men or women. A solution made from the roots was thought to cure venereal diseases. American Indians smelled the crushed leaves as a cure for a headache and made the raw root into a salve to relieve pain and swelling from rheumatism. A cough syrup was made from very sparse amounts of the boiled root. The root is very hot to the tongue and is somewhat narcotic.

Skunk cabbage was listed in the United States Pharmacopea from 1820 to 1882 and was used most often as relief from spasms or cramps or constrictions of any kind. It was used to treat bad coughs, asthma, lockjaw, epilepsy, and rheumatism.

COMMON NAME: **trillium**
FAMILY: Liliaceae (Lily)
GENUS: *Trillium*
SPECIES: *sessile*

DESCRIPTION: The petals of this perennial are brown or deep purple or sometimes even green and grow almost straight up from the stalk. They are nearly four times as long as they are wide, and the leaves are wide and a mottled green color. The entire plant is only four to twelve inches tall.

HABITAT: common in rich woods

BLOOMS: March through May

American Indians used this plant as an effective eye medicine. They either squeezed the juice directly onto their eyes or soaked the root and made an eye wash out of it. Indians also used the roots to ease the pain of childbirth. This practice was so common

that one species, *T. ovatum*, was also called birthroot.

Women commonly used this as a love potion. They would simply boil the root and then drop it in the food of the desired man. There is an old Indian story of a beautiful young girl who desired the chief's son for her husband, so she boiled the root of the trillium and took it to put in his food. On the way she tripped, and the root fell into the food of an ugly old man who promptly ate it and followed the unfortunate girl around for months begging her to marry him.

An old mountain superstition says if you pick the trillium, you will cause it to rain.

One common name, stinking Benjamin, refers to the red trillium, a close cousin of this plant, which does indeed have a most unpleasant odor.

Several varieties of trillium do well in a wildflower garden. *T. catesbaei* likes moist, acid soils, and *T. erectum* will thrive in a variety of soil conditions.

Trillium is a symbol for modest beauty.

WHITE FLOWERS

COMMON NAME: **trailing arbutus**
FAMILY: Ericaceae (Heath)
GENUS: *Epigaea*
SPECIES: *repens*

DESCRIPTION: This is a trailing vine often found most readily by its lovely, spicy scent. The flowers are white or sometimes pink, and the corolla is divided into five lobes. The leaves are oval, leathery, and covered with rust-colored hairs.

HABITAT: rocky, open woods

BLOOMS: February through May

Trailing arbutus has so caught the eye of man that it has been selected as the state flower of Massachusetts and the floral emblem of Nova Scotia. Another name that the plant often goes by is mayflower. The origin of that name has provoked a gentle controversy. Some claim that the name comes from the time of year the plant blooms, though in almost all areas it begins to bloom much earlier than May. Others believe the plant was named for the ship that brought the Pilgrims to America. According to one story, after a very long and cold winter, this was the first flower the Pilgrims found in the woods. The sight of it filled them with hope and good cheer, and they named the flower after the ship which had brought them to this new land. Another possibility is that this lovely little native wildflower was named for its slight resemblance to the hawthorne, which is called mayflower in England.

The more frquently used common name, trailing arbutus, has a rather complicated origin. Arbutus is from the Celtic word, *arboise*, which means "rough fruit." This name was apparently not given to our trailing arbutus, since it does not set any fruit. This was the name given to the English arbutus, an evergreen shrub with small white flowers similar to those of trailing arbutus.

Luckily, the origin of the botanical names is not nearly as complicated. *Epigaea* is from two Greek words, *epi*, meaning upon, and *gaea*, meaning earth. Taken together, they describe the trailing habits of this plant.

Although the Indians used trailing arbutus as an astringent and pioneer doctors used it as a diuretic, it is the beauty of the plant that contributed most to its current rarity. It was often dug or cut for bouquets and sold in the streets of New England towns. Today the flower is found on many states' rare and protected plant lists. Not only has the plant been extensively gathered, it also seems particularly sensitive to environmental disturbances, such as grazing and lumbering. Cultivation of the plant is, unfortunately, quite difficult because the trailing stems are very hard to transplant. Even if a stand is established, it usually takes three years or more before it graces the area with its exquisite, scented flowers.

COMMON NAME: **atamasco lily**
FAMILY: Amaryllidaceae (Amaryllis)
GENUS: *Zephyranthes*
SPECIES: *atamasco*

DESCRIPTION: The white lilylike flowers are sometimes tinged with pink and have six petals and six stamens. The leaves are the same height as the flower stalk (ten to twelve inches) and are narrow with sharp edges.

HABITAT: rich woods

BLOOMS: April through June

Although this plant is almost always referred to as a lily, boasting such names as zephyr lily, swamp lily, fairy lily, rain lily, and Easter lily, it is not a true lily, but a member of the Amaryllis family. The common and species name, atamasco, is from a Virginia Indian name, *attamusco*, which means "it is stained with red" and refers to the color of the buds and root stalks. The genus name is made up of two Greek words: *zephyr*, "northwest wind" (which presumably brought fair weather), and *anthos*, "flower." Taken together, *Zephyranthes* means flower of the north wind. In Greek mythology Zephyrus is the husband of Chloris, goddess of flowers. Not nearly so romantic is the name stagger-grass, given because the foliage and bulbs are poisonous. If even a small amount is eaten, it is often fatal. Many members of the Amaryllis Family are poisonous.

Atamasco lily is a good flower to put in any flower garden. The bulbs can be planted in either spring or fall, two inches deep and six inches apart, in full sun or partial shade.

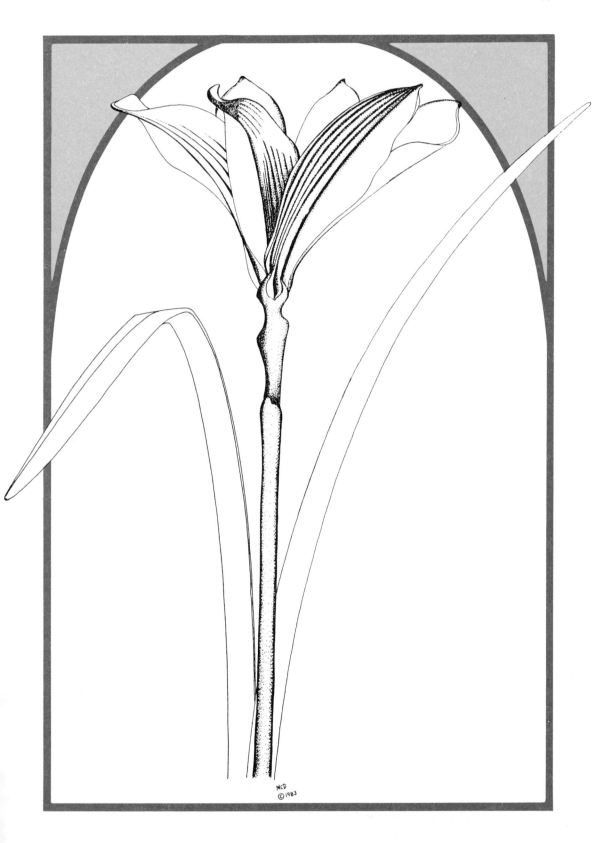

McD
©1983

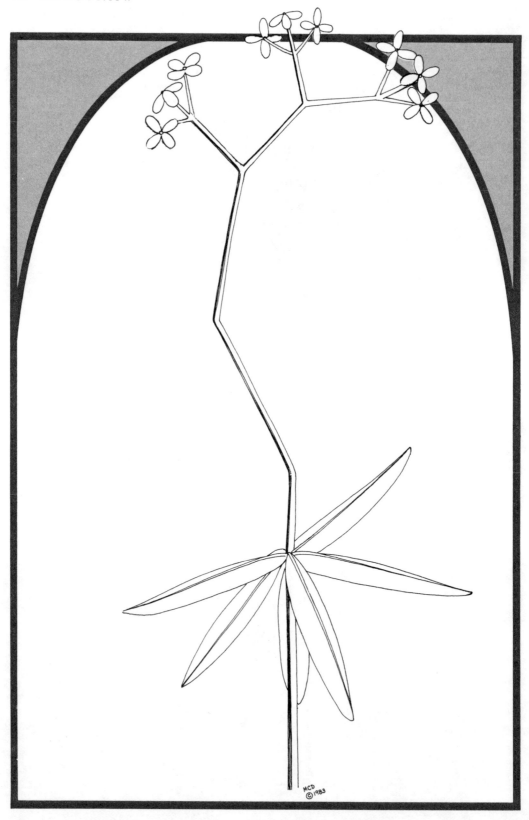

COMMON NAME: **bedstraw**
FAMILY: Rubiaceae (Bedstraw)
GENUS: *Galium*
SPECIES: *aparine*

DESCRIPTION: Bedstraw is often hard to see because the stems are very weak and lie close to the ground, almost like a vine. The leaves are long and narrow and occur in whorls. The flowers are white, and occur in terminal bundles. The stems are four-sided, and the entire plant is covered with bristly hairs.

HABITAT: common in woods, roadsides, meadows, and lawns

BLOOMS: April through July

There are approximately fifty-nine common names for this plant. One of the most often used is cleavers, from the fact that the bristles on the plant cling or cleave to animals and birds. Probably one reason the plant is so abundant is that the seeds are so easily carried from place to place by the wildlife. Other common names include goose grass (ducks and geese eat the seeds), catch weed, and scratch weed.

The name bedstraw has several possible origins. One explanation is that because the plant sticks so easily to clothing, it was possible to tell if the peasant boys had been tending sheep as they were supposed to or if they had been napping in the fields. Another possibility is that American pioneers used it as a mattress filler because the stems remained flexible even after they dried. The dried leaves smell somewhat like hay and were useful in repelling fleas from the beds. The generic name comes from the Greek word *gala*, meaning milk. Within the plant is an enzyme that causes milk to curdle, and in earlier times this plant was used in the cheese industry to hasten the curdling of milk.

Some members of this genus are European immigrants and others are true Americans. Bedstraw has always been connected with childbirth. It was said to have been the plant the Virgin Mary was lying on when she gave birth to the baby Jesus.

The medicinal and culinary uses of the plant are quite varied. The small dried fruits, if gathered when fully matured, were used as a coffee substitute. Since this plant is in the same family as the coffee tree, it serves as a better coffee substitute than most others. Tea made from the plant is reputed to be good for sunburn and for the complexion, and it was also reported to have the much sought after power to remove freckles.

A brew made from the leaves was drunk to help the blood coagulate. Old herb women considered cleavers, or bedstraw, to be a necessary part of the reducing diet. If gathered in early spring and cooked with mutton broth, bedstraw was said to make the figure look slim and young. If the truth were known, it was probably the tramping over the hillsides gathering the plant rather than the plant itself that really helped the figure more.

COMMON NAME: **bitterroot**
FAMILY: Portulacaceae (Purslane)
GENUS: *Lewisia*
SPECIES: *rediviva*

DESCRIPTION: The large white or pinkish flowers appear to be stemless, but they are actually on a stem one to two inches tall. The narrow, oblong leaves are thick and fleshy and grow in a rosette. The flower is composed of six to eight petallike sepals, twelve to eighteen small petals, and numerous stamens.

HABITAT: dry, rocky open areas

BLOOMS: April through July

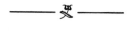

The flowering stem of bitterroot is so short that the blossom almost seems to sit on the ground. The large and showy blossom makes this a wonderful rock garden plant. It likes rocky, well-drained soil and will do well even in very poor soil. Although it does best started from seed, it is better to wait until fall to transplant it because the seedlings are difficult to care for.

This plant is also called the resurrection flower, because it has an amazing ability to rejuvenate after being dried out for a long time. It has been reported that the plant, having been pressed and dried for over a year, could be revived with a good soaking.

Bitterroot exhibits a somewhat unusual growth habit. The leaves first appear in the late fall, then die off when the plant blooms

in the spring and disappear by summer. With the arrival of cool weather in the fall, the leaves come out again. This tuft of leaves makes the plant easy to find in the early spring before it flowers. At this time of year the root has large amounts of starch in it. The bark can easily be peeled off, and then the root can be boiled, baked, or grated to add to flour or meal. Although the raw root is very bitter—hence the common name—this bitterness disappears after it is cooked. The young leaves are also tasty and nutritious. The roots were considered a great delicacy by pioneers and American Indians, although the pioneers would not gather them themselves, preferring to barter with the Indians for them. They were said to be especially good with venison gravy or huckleberry sauce.

Other common names are redhead Louisa or rockrose. The genus name is from the explorer, Meriwether Lewis (of Lewis and Clark fame), who collected the plant in what is now called the Bitterroot Valley in western Montana. Not only this valley, but also the Bitterroot Mountains and the Bitterroot River were named for this plant.

It is the state flower of Montana.

COMMON NAME: **bloodroot**
FAMILY: Papaveraceae (Poppy)
GENUS: *Sanguinaria*
SPECIES: *canadensis*

DESCRIPTION: The blossoms grow on a leafless stem, which rises from a rootstock that is usually one to two inches thick. The single blossom is white or sometimes pinkish and measures two inches across. The two sepals fall as the petals open. There are eight to sixteen petals and many stamens. The heart-shaped leaves are divided into five to nine lobes and continue to grow even after the petals fall. The bloodroot is the only known member of its genus.

HABITAT: rich woods and wood borders, low hillsides

BLOOMS: February through April

———— ✥ ————

The common name comes from the deep reddish brown or orange sap that comes from the roots. American Indians used this sap for war paint and to dye cloth and baskets. Pioneers used a drop of the sap on a lump of sugar as a cough medicine. The sap

had to be used sparingly when taken internally, though, because the roots are slightly poisonous. The rhizome was dried and sold as a stimiulant and was reported to be helpful in curing rattlesnake bites. The Indians used the juice as an insect repellent.

Another common name for this plant is red puccoon. This name also refers to the color of the juice that comes from the roots. The word "puccoon" is from an Indian word, *pak*, meaning blood and refers to plants used for dyeing. The generic name

comes from the Latin word *sanguis*, meaning blood. Bloodroot was often used as medicine for sick mules.

Since this is one of the first wildflowers to bloom in spring, it faces the hazards of a late frost, which will cause all the petals to fall off. The leaves stay curled around the base of the stem and unfurl only after the plant is pollinated, thus giving the plant some protection against cold. The leaves continue to grow until midsummer.

COMMON NAME: **chickweed**
FAMILY: Caryophyllaceae (Pink)
GENUS: *Stellaria*
SPECIES: *pubera*

DESCRIPTION: Chickweed's weak reclining stems grow compactly in the early part of the season and then become more loosely branched, often forming a dense mat. The leaves are bright green and ovate, or egg shaped. The white flowers have five sepals and what appears to be ten petals; actually they have five petals that are deeply divided. The flowers grow in the forks or at the ends of the stems.

HABITAT: This common plant is widely distributed, growing in most of the world, including some arctic regions. It is most often found growing in yards, gardens, woods, and wasteplaces.

BLOOMS: early spring through fall

Other common names for this plant include bird seed, starweed, and winterweed. That the seeds are eaten by several species of birds accounts for the name bird seed. The name winterweed probably came from the plant's ability to grow very early in the spring, even

when there is frost on the ground. The generic name *Stellaria* comes from the Latin word *stellar*, meaning starlike, and is descriptive of the starlike shape of the flowers.

Chickweed is hardy because it adjusts

easily to new soil conditions and its long growing season produces a great number of seeds each year.

The chickweed is regarded as a delicacy in Europe, because it is a very good substitute for spinach. When gathered in early spring, before flowering, it is more tender than any other wild green and is a good source of vitamins A and C.

Many ancient herbals listed chickweed as a poultice for boils and abscesses. In Elizabethan England it was used to reduce fever.

Chickweed has also been used in predicting the weather. If the chickweed blooms fully and boldly, the woods lore goes, there will be no rain for at least four hours. If the blossoms shut, get out your raincoat.

For positive identification of the plant, look through a magnifying glass at the hairs on the stems. A row of hairs goes up one side of the stem to a pair of leaves and then switches over and goes up the other side of the stem to the next pair of leaves and so on.

COMMON NAME: **daisy**
FAMILY: Compositae (Daisy)
GENUS: *Chrysanthemum*
SPECIES: *leucanthemum*

DESCRIPTION: The stem of the daisy is simple or slightly branched and smooth or slightly hairy. The leaves at the base are spoon shaped and deeply toothed. The flower heads are at the end of the stem and are solitary. They are one to two inches across and have twenty to thirty white ray flowers and bright yellow disks, or center flowers.

HABITAT: common in fields, meadows, waste places, and roadsides

BLOOMS: April through August

———— ✠ ————

The English had several common names for this plant. The name daisy comes from "day's eye" because the flower closes up at night. Other old English names include moondaisy, moon flower, or thunderflower (since it blooms in summer when thunder showers are common). It was connected with St. John and believed to hold the power to

keep away lightning. For this reason it was often hung indoors. Another common name for it in England is bruisewort, because the crushed leaves were often used for soothing bruised skin. It was believed that eating the roots of the daisy would stunt your growth. The stems and blossoms, when dried and then boiled, make a solution used to soothe chapped hands.

The daisy has often been used to tell fortunes. A simple way to tell the current state of your love life is to pick a daisy and then pick off the petals one by one, chanting "he loves me" with the first petal and "he loves me not" with the second and so on. The last petal tells the answer. The people of times past were actually quite shrewd. Since the daisy usually has an uneven number of petals, if you start with "he loves me," chances are pretty good that you will end up with "he loves me."

COMMON NAME: **Dutchman's breeches**
FAMILY: Papaveraceae (Poppy)
GENUS: *Dicentra*
SPECIES: *cucullaria*

DESCRIPTION: The stems and leaves of this plant arise from a pink, fleshy bulb. The flowers droop on an arched stem and are waxy, white, and have a yellow tip. The leaves are triangular in shape and are dissected many times. Each flower head has two inflated spurs that give it its unmistakeable shape.

HABITAT: rich woods and wood borders

BLOOMS: March through June

———— ✄ ————

The common name perfectly describes the shape of the spurs on the flower heads, which look like white pantaloons hanging upside down from the stem. The generic name *Dicentra* comes from the Latin word for hood and describes the two upper petals.

Another common name for this plant is blue staggers, which refers to the fact that it is poisonous. The plant contains alkaloids and has been known to kill cattle. The effects are not felt until two days after ingestion, and the symptoms include trembling, staggering, and labored breathing.

Although Dutchman's breeches will not stand being picked (it wilts easily), it looks lovely in a wildflower garden.

The plant is pollinated by bumblebees. However, the bees get short-changed, for their short tongues can reach the pollen, but not the nectar.

COMMON NAME: false Solomon's-seal
FAMILY: Liliaceae (Lily)
GENUS: *Smilacina*
SPECIES: *racemosa*

DESCRIPTION: The stem is strong and unbranched and arching, sometimes reaching a height of three feet. Leaves are alternately sessile and ribbed. A spike of white or yellow flowers grows at the end of the stem. It is easy to distinguish between this plant and the true Solomon's-seal when they are in bloom: true Solomon's-seal has blossoms hanging underneath the stem. Because the foliage is quite similar, it is difficult to tell them apart when they are not blooming.

HABITAT: found in rich woods

BLOOMS: May through June

This is one of the easiest plants to transplant and grow in your garden. It does fairly well both in strong sun and in dense shade. It can adapt to many types of soils, is resistant to many plant diseases, and propagates by rootstock or grows easily from seed.

Late in summer the plant produces mottled red berries, round and juicy. Enjoyed by the ruffled grouse and a few other species of birds, these berries are edible, but rather bitter.

The generic name comes from a Greek word that means rough or scraping and refers to the hairs on the stem. The species name, *racemosa*, comes from the Latin and is appropriate for this plant since the flowers occur in terminal clusters or racemes. The common name refers to its similarity to the true Solomon's-seal, but seems something of a misnomer, since there is nothing false about this plant. In fact, many people consider it much prettier than the true Solomon's-seal. It is also known as false spikenard.

COMMON NAME: **daisy fleabane**
FAMILY: Compositae (Daisy)
GENUS: *Erigeron*
SPECIES: *annuus*

DESCRIPTION: Fleabane can grow to heights of three to four feet or more. The stem is branched, and the leaves and the stem are covered with tiny hairs. The lower flowers are daisylike and white, sometimes tinged with pink or blue. There are usually several flowers to one stem.

HABITAT: very common in waste places, fields, and roadsides

BLOOMS: March through August

The generic name comes from two Greek words that mean spring and old man. The blossoms are said to resemble an old man's beard, and it blooms in the spring. The species name refers to the fact that it is an annual plant.

Fleabane was used by the early pioneers to keep away fleas and other unwanted insects. It was thought to be most effective when burned. It was also dried and stuffed in mattresses, but it is no longer believed to have any real insect repelling value.

The old English name for this plant is poor Robin's plantain, because the seeds were said to have been imported to Europe inside a stuffed bird.

An old superstition says if a pregnant woman wants to know the sex of her baby, she should plant a seed of the fleabane. If the flowers are tinged with pink, she will have a girl; if tinged with blue, a boy is on the way.

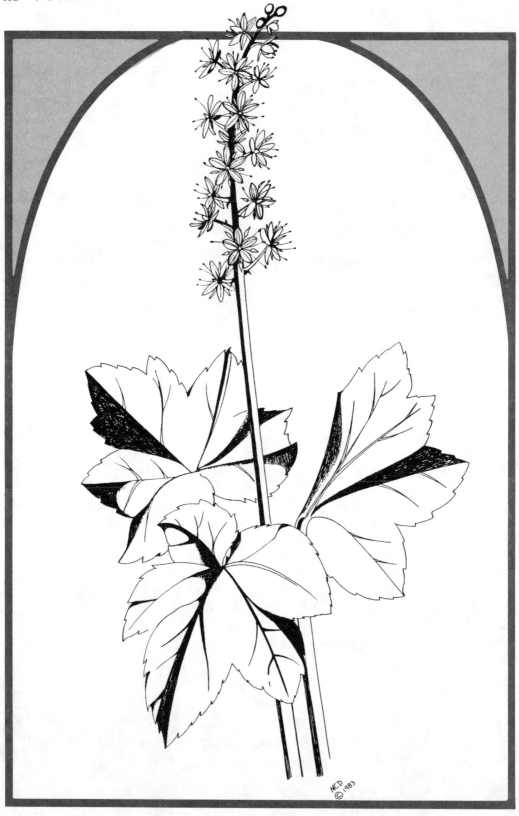

COMMON NAME: **foam flower**
FAMILY: Saxifragaceae (Saxifrage)
GENUS: *Tiarella*
SPECIES: *cordifolia*

DESCRIPTION: The leaves of this plant look much like red maple leaves and are almost always found at the base of the flowering stem. The flowers are on a long raceme and are white or sometimes tinged with pink. The stamens are extremely long. The height of the plant is six to twelve inches.

HABITAT: common in rich woods

BLOOMS: April through May

The common name for this plant comes from the delicate white flowers that look like foam. It got its generic name, meaning "little tiara" because the yellow pistils rise above the white petals like a golden crown, or, as the Greeks called them, tiaras. The Greeks often presented foam flowers as tokens of their love.

Once started, this plant will spread easily because it grows from underground runners and often forms colonies. It makes a fine groundcover, although it is not evergreen in all areas.

Other plants in this family include hydrangeas, gooseberries, and currants.

COMMON NAME: **ginseng**
FAMILY: Araliaceae (Ginseng)
GENUS: *Panax*
SPECIES: *quinquefolium*

DESCRIPTION: Ginseng flowers are greenish white and grow on an umbel that rises above a circle of large compound leaves. The flowers, only one-half inch in diameter with five petals, are arranged in clusters. The leaves in this species are divided into five leaflets. Crimson berries appear in July and August.

HABITAT: rich, deciduous woods

BLOOMS: May through August

In China ginseng is considered a "dose of immortality," and the Cherokee Indian name for it is "plant of life." Wherever it grows, ginseng has been revered for its medicinal value and held in awe for the amazing magical powers attributed to it. Few native wildflowers have been searched for so diligently or studied so extensively. Perhaps William Byrd in his *Histories of the Dividing Line Betwixt Virginia and North Carolina* has best described the magic that ginseng is thought to possess:

"... (ginseng roots) give uncommon warmth and vigour to the Blood, and frisks the Spirits. It cheers the Heart even of a Man that has a bad wife.... It helps the Memory.... In one word, it will make a Man live a great while,

and very well while he does live. ..."

It is not the blossom that is so attractive, for the flowers are small and insignificant. Nor is it the foliage, which is unremarkable. One must dig deeper to find out why the plant was accorded such value. It is the root that counts. Forked and gnarled, this root is "trouser-shaped" as the common name suggests (ginseng is a corruption of the Chinese word *Jin-chen*, which means "manlike" or "trouser-shaped"). The Iroquois Indian name for it is *garangtoging*, which means "child" and also refers to the shape. The generic name is from two Greek words: *pan*, meaning "all," and *akos*, meaning "cure," so the name literally means "cure all."

In China the ginseng root is used as a heart stimulant and has been prized for

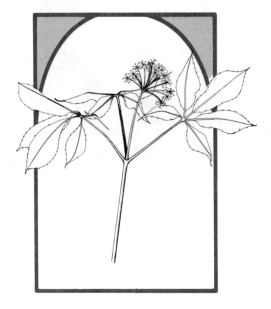

centuries as an aphrodisiac. For a long time only members of the Chinese nobility were allowed to use it, for it was thought too fine and expensive for commoners. At one point this was taken to the extreme, and a law was passed making it illegal for anyone other than the Emperor himself to collect ginseng.

American Indians used ginseng to treat coughs, headaches, and fevers and to strengthen mental processes. In America today it is mostly used as a general tonic. Research is under way to test the medicinal value of ginseng. Results so far have been interesting, to say the least. The root has been found to be beneficial to the endocrine glands, which help regulate hormonal flow. It is said to be especially beneficial to the aged and seems to help the body handle stress.

Because of its great popularity, ginseng is gathered extensively. In many states it is considered rare or threatened, and in some states it is protected as a renewable resource. In North America, ginseng is found growing in the Eastern deciduous forests. In Georgia alone the ginseng trade is more than $3 million annually. Most of the ginseng harvested in the United States goes to Hong Kong. With such vast amounts of the plant being harvested, some sort of regulation was necessary. To get export approval, the states must show some sort of ginseng regulation, and many states have passed laws. Representative of these is the 1979 Ginseng Protection Act in Georgia. According to this law, there is no quota on how much can be dug, but there are certain requirements which "sang diggers" (ginseng collectors) must meet. These are:

1. Registration with the State Game and Fish Department.
2. A tally of plants dug must be sent to this department.
3. The plant dug must have at least three prongs.
4. The berries of the plants must be planted to insure subsequent growth.

Why doesn't someone just cultivate such a desirable resource? Ginseng is easy to cultivate, transplants well, and will reproduce readily. The problem is that the cultivated roots seem not to have the "magic" found in the wild roots. The roots themselves look different—they are smoother, lacking the characteristic bumps found on the wild roots. American ginseng brokers will not accept these cultivated roots for export. This adds to the aura of mystery surrounding the plant. Ginseng, it seems, cannot be owned, but only respectfully borrowed to help man "live a great while, and very well while he does live."

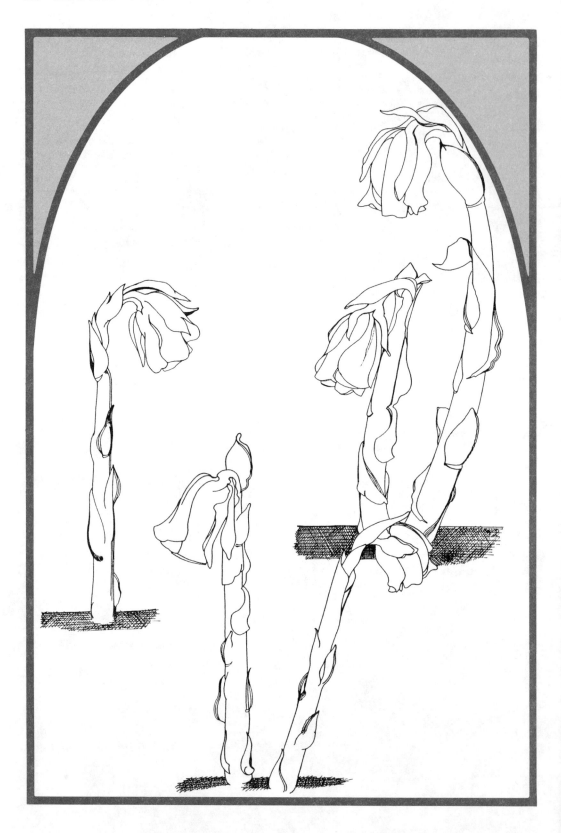

COMMON NAME: **Indian pipe**
FAMILY: Monotropaceae (Indian Pipe)
GENUS: *Monotropa*
SPECIES: *uniflora*

DESCRIPTION: This plant is easy to identify because it lacks chlorophyll and is therefore entirely white or translucent. The stem is scaly, with a single, nodding flower at the end. The blossom is regular and has four to five petals and ten stamens. There are few leaves, and these are alternate. It grows to three to nine inches.

HABITAT: moist, shady woods

BLOOMS: June through September

Indian pipe enjoys a symbiotic relationship with fungi that live on its roots, so it can exist without photosynthesizing. This means it has no need for chlorophyll, and it is white, standing out among other green plants. Because of its color and because it is cold to the touch and turns black when picked, it is also known by the names corpse plant, ice plant, and ghost flower. Since its single flower droops over, it resembles a peace pipe. The generic name is Greek for "one turn"; the plant turns to one side only. The species name refers to the single drooping flower. After the flower has set its seeds, it stands upright and may turn a light pink color.

The clear juice taken from the stem was used by American Indians as an eye medicine and was thought to sharpen vision.

COMMON NAME: **jimsonweed**
FAMILY: Solanaceae (Nightshade)
GENUS: *Datura*
SPECIES: *stramonium*

DESCRIPTION: This plant can grow to be four feet tall and is characterized by coarsely toothed leaves with spines and white or purplish trumpet-shaped flowers. The flowers are three to four inches long and form fruit in the late summer. The fruit is black with stickers or needles protruding from it.

HABITAT: common in waste places and roadsides

BLOOMS: June through September

The name jimsonweed is a corruption of Jamestown weed. It is so named because the plant was first found growing near that early New World settlement. It was also in Jamestown that the hallucinogenic effects of the fruit were discovered. A group of English soldiers on the way to Jamestown to quell an uprising ran short of food and supplies, so the soldiers gathered and ate the fruit of the jimsonweed. The soldiers heard sounds that no one else did and saw sights that were not there. American Indians often took carefully measured amounts of the plant to facilitate the coming of visions that would help them unravel the mysteries of the universe.

Jimsonweed was also used in soothing burned skin. Indians would heat the leaves and apply them directly to the burned area. Pioneers cooked the roots and leaves with hog fat and made a salve that was placed on burned skin. Asthma victims also benefited from the plant: the leaves, smoked like tobacco, helped to relieve labored breathing.

Other common names include thorn apple, in reference to the prickly fruit, and devil's trumpet, alluding to the shape of the flower.

This plant is poisonous, so be extremely careful in handling it.

COMMON NAME: **mayapple**
FAMILY: Berberidaceae (Barberry)
GENUS: *Podophyllum*
SPECIES: *peltatum*

DESCRIPTION: One of the easiest woods flowers to recognize, the mayapple has a pair of large umbrellalike leaves on a stem that can be as tall as eighteen inches. The leaves, attached to the stem nearly in the center, are coarsely toothed and divided into five to seven lobes. Only the stems that have two leaves bear flowers. The six sepals shed as the flower opens. There are six to nine white and waxy petals. The stamens and anthers are a conspicuous bright yellow. The fruit is a round yellow-green single berry the size and shape of a small lemon.

HABITAT: prefers a rich and moist environment

BLOOMS: April through June

The plant got its common name because the fruit ripens in May in many areas. The fruit is edible, but rather bitter. It was often used as flavoring or sometimes even to make marmalade. A Southern drink is made from wine, sugar, and the juice of the mayapple. Other common names include wild mandrake (although it is not a true mandrake), hog apple, wild lemon, umbrella leaf, and raccoon berry (because raccoons can often be seen eating the berries in the spring).

The generic name comes from a Greek word and means foot leaf. The species name means shield shaped. Both names refer to the large, conspicuous leaf.

Although several uses of the plant have been found, the root is poisonous, resulting in inflammation of eyes and skin. The Shawnee Indians used the boiled root as a very strong laxative.

The mayapple was once used to treat warts. Even today two drugs are taken from the mayapple plant. One, called podophyllin, is a strong cathartic. The other, peltatine, is being used in experiments dealing with cancer.

Beware of moving this plant. Not only should it not be moved for ecological reasons, but also because an old mountain superstition says that a girl who pulls up the root of the mayapple will soon become pregnant. The true mandrake, which looks similar to this plant, was sold to women as an assurance of fertility.

COMMON NAME: **partridgeberry**
FAMILY: Rubiaceae (Madder)
GENUS: *Mitchella*
SPECIES: *repens*

DESCRIPTION: The leaves are smooth and shiny, round and opposite on long, slender trailing stems. The stems are about four to twelve inches long, and the leaves are only one-half inch long. The small, white-fringed blossoms occur in pairs, are united at the base, and smell a bit like lilac. The flowers are followed by brightly colored red berries, which often stay until the next blooming season. The leaves are evergreen. The stems often take root at the nodes and form a mat.

HABITAT: common in woods

BLOOMS: May through July

This is one of the best plants to use in home terrariums, as it transplants easily and thrives in a moist environment. In a wildflower garden it does very well if given sufficient shade and moisture. It does particularly well if packed in leaf mold under rhododendrons or azaleas. It grows quickly, but rarely becomes a pest.

The common name is from the fact that the berries are eaten by several species of birds, including grouse, quail, and wild turkey. The generic name is from John Mitchell (1680–1768), who developed a method of treating yellow fever victims and saved thousands of lives during the Philadelphia epidemic. The species name is

especially appropriate, because it means trailing or creeping and describes the growth habits of the plant. Other common names include twinberry, squawberry, and checkerberry.

Cherokee Indian women made a tea from this plant and drank it for weeks before having a baby. They believed it would hasten childbirth and make labor easier. The tea was also used to treat coughs and colds.

Although the flowers grow in pairs, they are not alike. One has a long pistil and short stamens, and the opposite flower has a short pistil and long stamens. This is called dimorphism, and because of this no flower can fertilize itself; all flowers must be cross-fertilized by insects. The flowers are united at the base and form a single berry in the fall. Both flowers must be fertilized to get a single healthy berry.

COMMON NAME: **pipsissewa**
FAMILY: Ericaceae (Heath)
GENUS: *Chimaphila*
SPECIES: *maculata*

DESCRIPTION: The evergreen leaves are whorled and dark green with a white midrib. The white flowers, measuring two-thirds inch across, rise above the leaves about eight inches.

HABITAT: common in all types of woods

BLOOMS: May through July

Because this plant is green throughout the winter the generic name is appropriate: it is from two Greek words, *phileo*, meaning to love, and *cheima*, meaning winter. Together they mean winter loving.

The common name is a Creek Indian word meaning "juice breaks down stone in bladder into small pieces" and refers to their belief that the plant could cure bladder or

kidney stones. The Shawnee Indians used the plant to make a tea to cure consumption. The Pennsylvania Germans believed it would induce sweating to break a chill, and some American mountaineers used it to cure urinary disturbances. An extract made from this plant was a common ingredient in rootbeer.

A native of North America, Asia, and

Europe, it is often found in the woods under evergreen trees and is pollinated by several kinds of bees and flies. Other common names are king's cure, noble pine, love-in-winter, ground holly, pine tulip, and bittersweet.

This plant seems to actually benefit from light forest fires, as seedling reproduction usually increases after a fire.

COMMON NAME: **pokeweed**
FAMILY: Phytolaccaceae (Pokeweed)
GENUS: *Phytolacca*
SPECIES: *americana*

DESCRIPTION: The stems of this plant are large and tinged with red, often growing to heights of ten feet or more. The leaves are soft and pliable. The small white flowers and the dark purple berries are borne on erect racemes.

HABITAT: common in dry areas or disturbed places

BLOOMS: May through October

Probably no other plant gets as much attention in the spring as does the pokeweed, or poke sallet, as many of the mountain people call it. The young shoots are collected and then cooked like greens. An old mountain recipe says to wash and cook the stems and leaves together and to boil and drain them several times. Eating poke sallet in the spring is said to revive the blood, and since it is full of vitamin C and iron, it could be quite beneficial. However, once the plant gets about three feet high, it should not be eaten, because the roots and berries are poisonous. The old fashioned antidote for poke poisoning is to drink lots

of vinegar and eat a pound of lard! This is incentive enough not to eat the pokeweed if you have any doubts as to whether or not it is the right time to eat the plant.

Besides being an excellent spring vegetable, pokeweed has many other virtues. The Algonquin Indians called the plant *puccoon*, which means "plant used for staining or dyeing." This also accounts for the common name inkberry. The berries are dark purple and make an excellent dye. An old mountain custom was to wear a string of poke berries around your neck to avoid catching a contagious disease. Although the root is poisonous, if made into a salve, it is

useful for soothing burns and sores that do not heal easily. A concoction made from the roots and leaves was given as a tonic to chickens when they seemed sluggish. The berries are eaten by robins, woodpeckers, flickers, and several other species of birds.

In the presidential campaign of 1844, James K. Polk and his supporters wore pokeberry leaves as a campaign symbol.

COMMON NAME: **field pussytoes**
FAMILY: Compositae (Daisy)
GENUS: *Antennaria*
SPECIES: *plantaginifolia*

DESCRIPTION: The many varieties of pussytoes are often difficult to tell apart. In general, pussytoes have relatively large basal leaves with smaller leaves occuring alternately up the stem. There are mats of hair along the stem and underneath the leaves. The numerous flower heads are white or off-white. The plant may grow as tall as eighteen inches.

HABITAT: prefers fields and pastures

BLOOMS: March through July

Anyone who has ever held a kitten and touched its tiny paws will know immediately where this plant's common name comes from. The flower heads are so soft and dainty that they really do look like a kitten's paw. The generic name refers to the feathery seeds: the Greeks thought these seed pods looked like the antennae of a butterfly. The species name refers to the plantainlike leaves characteristic of this species.

Pussytoes are most often found growing in clumps with very few other plants growing close by. This is because the plant puts out a substance that other plants cannot tolerate. This substance, called a growth inhibitor, assures each pussytoes plant an ample supply of water and nutrients. This kind of growth pattern is commonly found in desert plants, which

must compete strongly for all nutrients.

Old country folks used the flower heads as a shampoo to get rid of lice and also packed them away with winter clothes to keep away moths. Other common names are everlasting, mouse ear, and ladies' tobacco.

COMMON NAME: **Queen Anne's lace**
FAMILY: Umbelliferae (Parsley)
GENUS: *Daucus*
SPECIES: *carota*

DESCRIPTION: The branched, hairy leaves measure two to eight inches long and closely resemble the parsley leaf. The small flowers are in dense heads, three or four inches across, and are white or yellowish except for the very center flower, which is often deep rose or purple. The height of the plant is one to three feet.

HABITAT: common in dry, open places or thin woods

BLOOMS: May through October

Queen Anne's lace, or wild carrot, is a flower that takes care of itself. During wet weather the stem becomes very soft and flexible an inch or two below the flower head. This causes the head to bend over, and the pollen is thus protected from the rain. The older plants that have already lost their pollen remain standing up straight even during the heaviest downpour. The plant has a very strong odor; it is not particularly pleasing to people, but is apparently attractive to a number of insects, for it never lacks pollinators.

Queen Anne's lace is a member of the parsley family, about which legends and superstition abound. Crowns of parsley were worn by the victors of the Grecian games. The Greeks also used parsley on graves to assure their loved ones that they were still remembered. One old legend says that parsley takes a long time to germinate, because it goes to the devil nine times before appearing above ground. Those who wanted to slight the devil and raise parsley in a hurry would plant it on Good Friday. To transplant parsley would bring years of bad luck.

Parsley had a reputation for being an antidote for poison, and to put it on a plate of food served to a guest was a token of

MCD
©1983

trust. An old woodsman's trick, which has been supported by modern medicine, is to grate the root of Queen Anne's lace and apply it to burns. Since the root contains carotin, when mixed with oil it really does have healing powers.

Queen Anne's lace also had a reputation for curing internal parasites, such as worms. Both the grated root and the juice from the stem can be eaten. Although the blossoms usually were not eaten, eating the center purple floret was once thought to cure epilepsy.

Those who did not need the magical or medicinal powers of the bee's nest or bird's nest root, as Queen Anne's lace was sometimes called, often used the flower heads in dried flower arrangements.

The common name Queen Anne's lace comes from the frilly blossoms, which look like the lacy layers of a headdress fit for a queen. One story says that a queen was making lace when she pricked her finger. The center purple floret on the flower represents a drop of blood from the queen's finger.

COMMON NAME: **rattlesnake plantain**
FAMILY: Orchidaceae (Orchid)
GENUS: *Goodyera*
SPECIES: *pubescens*

DESCRIPTION: Nestled down in the dead leaves of the woods, the oval-shaped, white-veined leaves of rattlesnake plantain are beautiful even when the plant is not in bloom. The flowers are small, white, and arranged on a hairy stalk that is eighteen inches tall.

HABITAT: common in both moist and dry woods

BLOOMS: July through August

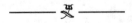

This plant is named for John Goodyer, a seventeenth-century botanist. The common name comes from the unusual markings on the leaves, markings that resemble those on the skin of a rattlesnake. The name rattlesnake could also refer to the stalk of

white flowers, which looks like the rattles on a rattlesnake's tail.

Although not a true plantain, the common name was given to this plant because of the way the leaves grow in a basal

rosette, as in the plantains. The species name *pubescens* means hairy and refers to the stem.

American Indian women believed if they rubbed their bodies with this plant it would cause their husbands to love them more.

The Orchids were named for an unfortunate youth, Orchis, who was the son of a nymph and a satyr. Attending a festival one evening and having indulged in too much wine, he let his passions get the best of him and approached a priestess and grabbed her. The horrified crowd tore him apart. His father begged the gods to make him whole again, but the gods refused, saying that it was a deadly sin to attack a priestess. However, taking some pity on the father, they did allow that his son's death should bring some beauty to the world and made the Orchids from the remains of his body.

COMMON NAME: **rue anemone**
FAMILY: Ranunculaceae (Buttercup)
GENUS: *Anemonella*
SPECIES: *thalictroides*

DESCRIPTION: This woodland plant grows to a height of only eight inches. The leaves are divided into three lobes, which are rounded at the tip and are found toward the top of the flowering stem. The blossoms are small and white or pink, have five to ten sepals, and have no petals. There are two to three blossoms on one stem.

HABITAT: common throughout in woods or woody thickets

BLOOMS: March through May

This plant was named for its "look-a-likes." The generic name comes from *Anemone*, or the windflower, which its blossoms closely resemble. The species name is from the meadow rue, which the foliage of the rue anemone closely resembles.

The rue anemone was thought to have great healing powers and was adopted by the Persians as a symbol of disease. Although no special powers are attributed to it today, many of the species do have a substance in their juice that supposedly helps cure many foot disorders.

This delicate plant is easy to grow in a wildflower garden. It needs light shade and rich soil.

COMMON NAME: **shortia**
FAMILY: Diapensiaceae (Diapensia)
GENUS: *Shortia*
SPECIES: *galacifolia*

DESCRIPTION: The leaves of shortia are rounded, shiny, and evergreen and look very much like those of galax, though there are distinct veins present in the former. There is a single white (or sometimes pink), bell-shaped flower, which is borne on a leafless stalk. It grows quite low to the ground, reaching a height of only one to three inches.

HABITAT: rich, moist woods, especially along streambanks

BLOOMS: March through April

This very rare, lovely flower is native only to seven counties in Georgia, South Carolina, and North Carolina. In other areas where it is found, it has been transplanted. Ten other species of the genus grow in Japan, China, and Formosa.

Shortia was discovered by Andre Michaux in the North Carolina mountains in 1788. Michaux put a specimen of the plant in a herbarium in Paris, where it was found and named by Asa Gray in the 1840s. He named it *Shortia* after Charles W. Short, a Kentucky doctor and botanist who lived in the early 1800s. Dr. Short was an avid plant collector and had an herbarium of 15,000 species, which he donated to the

Philadelphia Academy of Natural Science. Asa Gray and other botanists searched diligently for *Shortia*, but were unable to find it. Not until 1877 was it rediscovered; George Hyams, a 17-year-old boy, found it growing in McDowell County, North Carolina. Soon after this a similar species, *Shortia uniflora*, was found growing in Japan.

The species name, *galacifolia*, refers to the galaxlike leaves. Another common name frequently used is Oconee bells, named for the bell shape of the flower and the fact that it was found growing in the Oconee area of the Appalachian mountains.

Shortia can be grown in the garden,

either in pots or in shady areas under rhododendrons or azaleas. It prefers soil rich in humus. It can be propagated by dividing the plant after flowering or by growing cuttings in sand and peat in the early fall.

COMMON NAME: soapwort
FAMILY: Caryophyllaceae (Pink)
GENUS: *Saponaria*
SPECIES: *officinalis*

DESCRIPTION: Clusters of pink or white flowers are found on two or three branches of this rather ragged-looking plant. The petals have scalloped edges and are reflexed back. The stem, which may grow as tall as two feet or more, is smooth and swollen at the joints; the leaves are ribbed, entire, and opposite.

HABITAT: waste places and roadsides

BLOOMS: July through September

If you bruise the leaves of this plant and add them to water, the result is a delightful, bubbly lather. This characteristic of the plant has been known at least since the Middle Ages, because it was recorded that friars brought seeds of the plant with them to England from France and Germany at that time. They believed that soapwort had been sent to them by God to keep them clean and healthy, and it was frequently found growing close to monasteries and hospitals.

Soapwort was found to be especially useful in cleaning and lightly bleaching fabric. The leaves were added to water and used to whiten the fabric before it was printed. Later, soapwort was planted close to textile mills, and it soon became affectionately known as fuller's herb (a fuller was one who worked with cloth). Soapwort was planted in Colonial gardens for similar reasons. It was quite effective in restoring the color and sheen to old china and glass, and a solution made from the leaves is still used for this purpose today.

Because the blossoms have a pleasantly strong smell, the flower was often planted along poor streets in cities to hide the stench from improper sanitation practices. In this context, soapwort was often sarcastically referred to as "London Pride."

The cleansing property of the leaves was

MCD
©1983

also used to treat rashes such as poison ivy and other skin disorders. Modern pharmaceutical research has found chemicals within the plant that are useful in treating syphillis, jaundice, and liver problems. The plant is somewhat poisonous, however, and caution is advised when using it for medicinal purposes. Its poisons did not stop medieval brewers from using the leaves to

put a good head on a mug of beer, though.

The genus name is from the Latin word *sapon*, which means soap. Another common name is bouncing Bet. It was thought that the white reflexed petals of the blossom looked like the rear view of a washerwoman (named Bet, of course) with her petticoats all pinned up.

COMMON NAME: **Solomon's-seal**
FAMILY: Liliaceae (Lily)
GENUS: *Polygonatum*
SPECIES: *biflorum*

DESCRIPTION: Because of the zigzag stem and the arrangement of the leaves, this plant can easily be confused with false Solomon's-seal. When they are in bloom it is much easier to tell them apart. The flowers on this plant are greenish white and hang down under the stem in pairs, while false Solomon's-seal has a spike of flowers at the end of the stem. Solomon's-seal grows to a height of eight to thirty-six inches. The leaves are pale green and downy underneath.

HABITAT: prefers dry woods and a slightly acid soil

BLOOMS: May through June

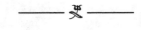

The generic name comes from the Greek words *poly* and *gonum*, meaning "many jointed," and refers to the number of joints in the rootstock. The species name refers to the flowers, which hang down from the stem in pairs.

The most widely accepted origin of the common name is that it comes from the scars on the rootstock, which are somewhat signet shaped and resemble a royal seal. The name Solomon is for King Solomon, the tenth century B.C. king of Israel who was

famed for his wisdom. King Solomon was thought to have known much about medicinal herbs, and it was believed that he placed his seal of approval on this plant.

American Indians crushed the roots of Solomon's-seal to make flour or made pickles out of sections of the root. Both the roots and the shoots are edible if gathered in the early spring. When the root of the plant is crushed and applied to a wound, it is said to take the black and blue out of a bruise. A tea made from the crushed leaves was used as a contraceptive.

The language of Solomon's-seal is concealment and discretion. If sent between two lovers, it would mean "our secret will be kept."

This plant does very well in a woodland wildflower garden. During the winter it appreciates a covering of pine needles or oak leaves. It grows best in a soil with pH of 4.5 to 5.0.

Just as you can tell the age of a tree by counting the rings, so you can tell the age of a Solomon's-seal by counting the number of stem scars on the roots. There is one circle for each year.

A drawing of Solomon's-seal was found in a sixteenth-century herbal. The plant was known as *Sigillum benedictae virginis*, or seal of the Blessed Virgin. It was thought that you could rid a house of snakes and spiders by spreading this plant over the floor.

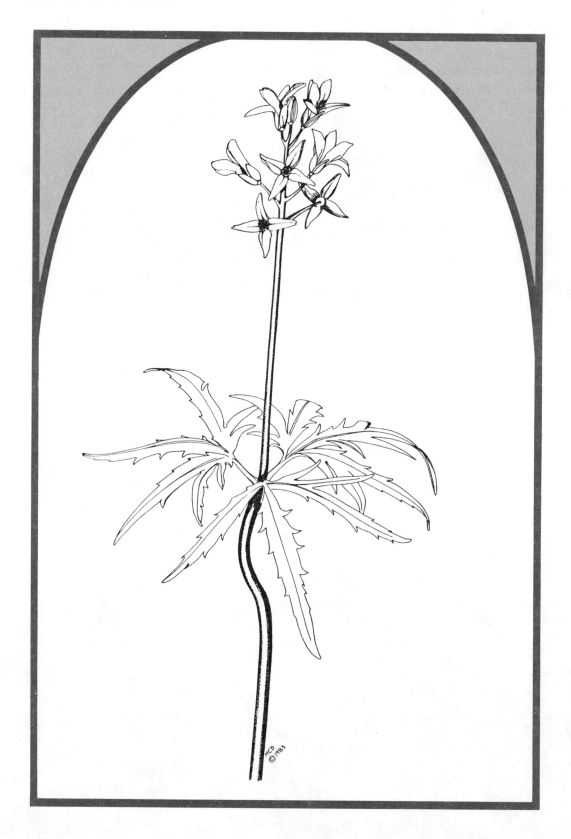

COMMON NAME: **toothwort**
FAMILY: Cruciferae (Mustard)
GENUS: *Dentaria*
SPECIES: *laciniata*

DESCRIPTION: Toothwort has a whorl of three leaves, each of which is divided into three segments near the top of the stem. Each leaf segment is sharply toothed. The flowers are pinkish white, and there are several flowers to each stem, which grows eight to sixteen inches tall. Basal leaves are absent when it is blooming.

HABITAT: prefers rich, moist environment

BLOOMS: March through June

Other common names for this plant include lady's smocks, crinkleroot, milkmaids, cut leaf, pepperwort, and pepper-root. The root, which has a peppery flavor, can be eaten as a woodland nibble or it can be diced and put into salads.

The generic name is based on the Latin word meaning tooth and refers to the white toothlike projections on the rootstock. The doctrine of signatures held that this plant would relieve toothaches, because of the rootstock's resemblance to teeth.

Toothwort grows in rich woods and along streambanks. Though the flowers are small, it is valued in wildflower gardens for its early spring color.

COMMON NAME: **watercress**
FAMILY: Cruciferae (Mustard)
GENUS: *Nasturtium*
SPECIES: *officinale*

DESCRIPTION: The flowers are very small and white, with four petals as is characteristic of the family. There are several small white roots, and the leaves, which measure one to six inches across, are succulent and have three to nine leaflets. The seed pods are long and slender.

HABITAT: running water in creeks and streams

BLOOMS: April through June

This European member of the mustard family shares the generic name *Nasturtium* with the garden flower from a different family. They share this name because both plants' leaves have a sharp, biting taste. The name *Nasturtium* is from Latin and means "twisted nose," referring to the acrid taste. Another common name is teng-tongue. The bright green leaves and young stems, which are high in vitamin C, are one of the most delicious of all wild plants and are used in salads and as garnishes. "Cress butter" is made by mixing sweet butter and chopped watercress and is similar to parsley butter.

Although watercress is much sought after for its delightful taste, be careful: it often grows in contaminated water.

Fishermen are always glad to see a stand of watercress, because it is a favorite hiding place for trout and because it forms an excellent breeding ground for those things that trout like to eat, such as freshwater shrimp and snails.

Watercress has been used and eaten for centuries. Romans used it to "quiet deranged minds."

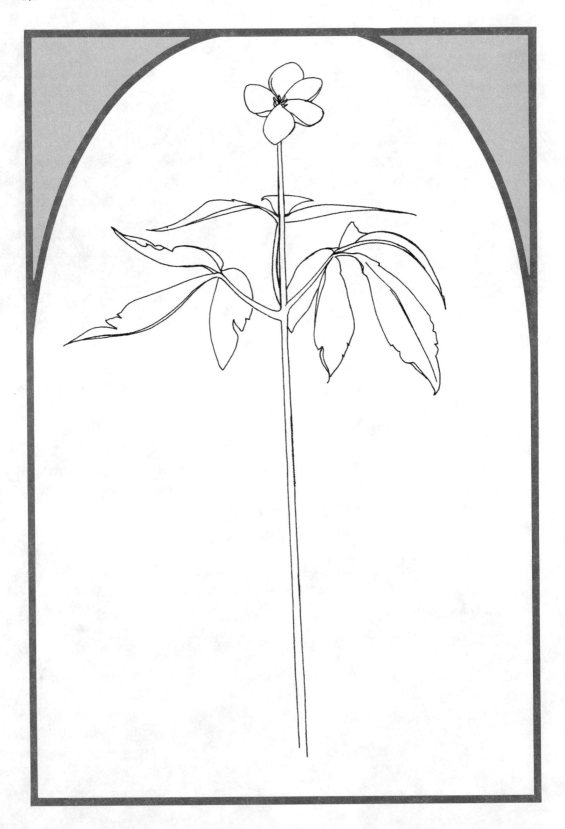

COMMON NAME: **wood anemone**
FAMILY: Ranunculaceae (Buttercup)
GENUS: *Anemone*
SPECIES: *quinquefolia*

DESCRIPTION: The flowers of this delicate woods plant are solitary and appear before the leaves do. The most conspicuous parts of the blossom are the white petallike sepals. These sepals may be tinged with pink or sometimes blue. The stems are four to eight inches tall. The leaves are whorled and are divided into three sharply toothed leaflets.

HABITAT: common in woods, thickets, and clearings

BLOOMS: March through May

Legend tells us the original home of this flower was Mount Olympus, where the prevailing winds blow. The name anemone was from the Greek god of the winds, Anemos, and these flowers herald his coming in the spring. Pliny wrote that only the wind can open the anemone. Another legend says that Venus was crying in the woods for her lost lover, Adonis, and everywhere her tears fell, an anemone grew—a story that seems to suit this fragile-looking plant.

The Romans made much ado of picking the first anemones in the spring. Saying prayers while picking them, they believed, would guard against disease in the coming year. A typical prayer was chanted, imploring the god to safeguard the individual.

In the Near East people connected the anemones with sickness and would hold their breath and run past places where the plant grew. The Chinese call it the death plant and plant it on the graves of their loved ones.

The species name means five leaves; actually, though, it is a misnomer, since the leaves are simply deeply divided and not separate leaves.

Other common names for this plant include windflower, nimbleweed, mayflower, and woodflower. The generic name came from the Sanskrit word *aniti*, meaning "to breathe."

Wood anemone is a good specimen for shady gardens or rock gardens, as it will grow in a variety of conditions. It does well either planted at the base of trees in groups or scattered throughout a shady area or along a path.

COMMON NAME: **yarrow**
FAMILY: Compositae (Daisy)
GENUS: *Achillea*
SPECIES: *millefolium*

DESCRIPTION: The grey-green leaves are finely dissected, fernlike, and aromatic, especially when crushed. The flowers grow in clusters at the top of the stem and are whitish. They are composed of four to six ray flowers surrounding a small, dense head of disk flowers. The plant stands one to three feet fall.

HABITAT: roadsides and dry fields

BLOOMS: June through September

The best known medicinal use of yarrow was to staunch the flow of blood from a wound. Modern testing has proven that this was more than superstition; chemicals in the plant are effective in clotting blood. The leaves were ground up, boiled, and made into a salve and applied to wounds. A number of additional common names for yarrow refer to this beneficial trait: soldier's woundwort, nosebleed, bloodwort, staunchgrass, and staunchweed.

The genus name, *Achillea*, is from the Greek hero Achilles. According to legend he always carried the plant with him to treat wounded soldiers during the Trojan Wars. Perhaps due to this legend, the language of yarrow is war. The species name, *millefolium*, is literally translated to mean "a thousand leaves" and is descriptive of the feathery foliage.

Yarrow's magical healing powers were not restricted to staunching the flow of blood. Concoctions made from the plant were reputed to cure quite a variety of ailments. American Indians used it to soothe bruises and burns and cure earaches. Pioneers found chewing on the leaves would help

MCD

settle an upset stomach or help regulate the menstrual flow. Gerard (see downy false foxglove) wrote that chewing on the green leaves would help a toothache. The leaves, dried and made into a tea, were effective in treating chills, fever, and gout, and if applied to the head, were beneficial to the hair and scalp. The leaves also were ground into a salve and used to put on rashes and soothe nipples sore from breastfeeding.

Not all of yarrow's powers were thought to be good. Another common name for the plant was devil's plaything, because it was thought to have been used by Satan for casting spells. Yarrow, wrapped in flannel and placed under a pillow, was thought to bring prophetic dreams about love matters to the person sleeping on the pillow. If, however, that person dreamed of cabbages, it meant the coming of bad luck.

Lys de Bray, in her book *The Wild Garden*, says it's good to grow yarrow in an herb garden because it "... strengthens its neighbors, making them disease-resistant, and intensifying the strength and yield of the aromatic oils from the culinary herbs." Luckily for the enthusiastic herbalist, yarrow is easy to grow and almost always flourishes. Propagation can be done either by division of the plant or by sowing seeds; it also self-sows.

Although yarrow has extensive medicinal value, a Chinese proverb probably would influence more people to eat it than any health guide could. This proverb says that yarrow brightens the eyes and promotes intelligence.

YELLOW FLOWERS

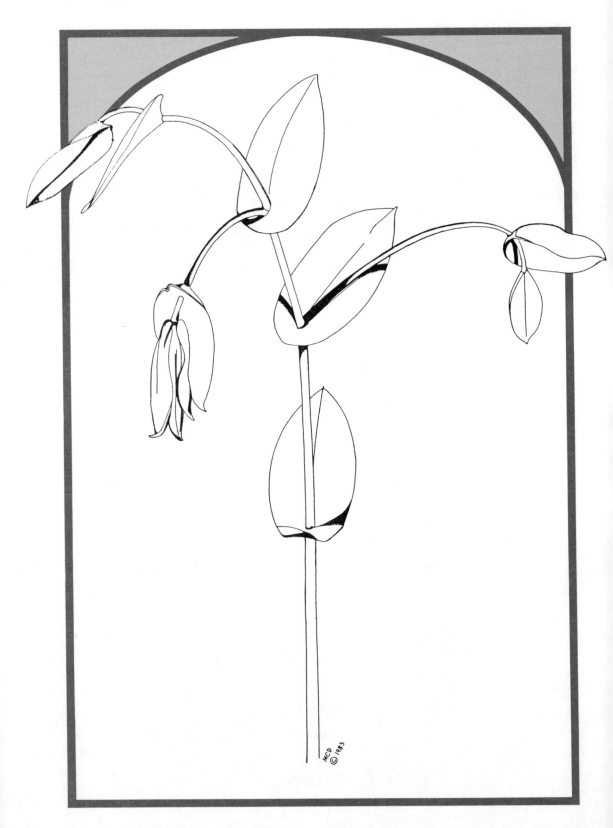

COMMON NAME: **bellwort**
FAMILY: Liliaceae (Lily)
GENUS: *Uvularia*
SPECIES: *perfoliata*

DESCRIPTION: Even when in full bloom, the yellow bellwort blossoms look almost closed; sometimes you must look carefully to find them. Both the petals and sepals are the same size and color. The leaves clasp the stem. After flowering, the stem continues to grow, sometimes to a height of ten to twelve inches.

HABITAT: moist woods

BLOOMS: April through June

Although many common plant names end in "wort," there is some discrepancy as to what that suffix actually means. Some authors suggest that it comes from the word *wyrt* and means "root" or "herb." Other authors claim that "wort" meant that that particular plant had medicinal or culinary value.

The bellwort boasts kitchen and sickroom value. It was once thought to be an effective cure for throat problems, according to the doctrine of signatures. The earliest herbalists thought the blossoms of the bellwort looked like the uvula, that funny-looking pink thing that hangs down from the soft palate in the back of the mouth.

As with many other spring wildflowers, the young shoots are quite tasty and are often picked and cooked like asparagus.

The common name, of course, comes from the bell-like shape of the blossoms.

MCD
© 1983

COMMON NAME: black-eyed Susan
FAMILY: Compositae (Daisy)
GENUS: *Rudbeckia*
SPECIES: *hirta*

DESCRIPTION: This plant is inaccurately named, since the centers are actually reddish brown and not a true black. Its sturdy, hairy stems grow to a height of one to three feet. The yellow flower heads measure two to three inches across. The leaves are lance shaped and are seven to eight inches long.

HABITAT: common in fields, roadsides, and other open places

BLOOMS: May through September

A native of North America, black-eyed Susan comes from the plains and prairies of the Midwest. This genus is named for a Swedish botanist, Olaf Rudbeck, who taught botany to the "father of modern botany," Caroleus Linnaeus.

Because the black-eyed Susan is shunned by all types of livestock, a profusion of the plant indicates overgrazing and poor soil conditions, since it will take over when other plants have been grazed out. Although dependent on bees, wasps, butterflies, beetles, flies, and a variety of other insects for pollination, the plant has nevertheless developed a method of keeping away unwanted pests, such as ants. The stems are covered with tiny barbs which make it impossible, or at least very uncomfortable, for ants to crawl up.

Horticulturists who admired the black-eyed Susan have hybridized it to form the gloriosa daisy.

The black-eyed Susan is a very hardy plant and usually does quite well in a wildflower garden. It prefers a dry, acid soil and bright sun.

It was effectively used to treat skin infections and has been found to contain antibodies.

This is the state flower of Maryland.

COMMON NAME: **buttercup**
FAMILY: Ranunculaceae (Buttercup)
GENUS: *Ranunculus*
SPECIES: *acris*

DESCRIPTION: Arising from a short tuberous root, the stem of this plant grows to a height of only eight inches. There are five yellow petals and numerous stamens. Unlike many species of buttercups, this species has stems that stand erect.

HABITAT: common in both wet and dry woods and open places

BLOOMS: March through April

The tiny, innocent buttercup at some point acquired the reputation of causing lunacy and was called the "crazy weed" by many country folk. To hold the flower next to your neck on a night when the moon is full, or simply to smell the flower, were said to drive you insane. Although there has never been an official report as to anyone's actually losing his mind because of the buttercup, many species are poisonous and will severely irritate the skin. Since the juice of the buttercup quickly raises a blister on the skin, it was often used by beggars in an attempt to create more sympathy. One species of the buttercup was even used in poison arrows. If taken internally, it will cause stomach inflammation. Animals are also affected, especially cattle. A cow that eats the plant produces bitter milk tinged with red. The poisonous materials in the buttercups evaporate quickly and are not dangerous when dried.

More than 275 species of buttercups grow worldwide. Since many of these grow in bogs or moist areas, this could account for the generic name. The word *Ranunculus* is Latin, meaning "little frog." Another explanation for the frog name is that the seeds from the buttercup resemble a small frog. The common name is from the color of the petals. Other common names include blister plant (from the poisonous properties), gold knots, and meadow ranunculus.

Another story of how the buttercup got the name *Ranunculus* was that this was the name of a Libyan boy who could sing very beautifully. He always wore green and gold silk, and he was constantly singing. One day while he was singing in the woods, the wood nymphs heard him. To get some peace and quiet, they turned him into a green and gold flower, which we call the buttercup today.

Ar old custom is to hold the blossom under your chin: if your chin shines yellow, you love butter.

COMMON NAME: **cattail**
FAMILY: Typhaceae (Cattail)
GENUS: *Typha*
SPECIES: *latifolia*

DESCRIPTION: The individual cattail flowers are very small and almost indistinguishable. They cluster on a clublike stalk, with the yellow male, or staminate, flowers on the top and the densely packed female, or pistillate, flowers directly underneath.

In this species there is no break between the male and female portions of the stem. After the pollen has been shed, the male flowers drop off the stalk. The leaves are flat and swordlike and are taller than the flowering stalk. It can grow to a height of three to nine feet.

HABITAT: fresh-water marshy areas

BLOOMS: May through July

This plant, which is common in marshy or bog areas, serves as roosting cover for game birds. The cattail is so essential to the birds that in a given area, the number of cattails present actually determines the number of pheasants that will winter in that area.

The plant is most conspicuous in early spring when the seeds develop downy parachutes. These downy seeds were used for stuffing in quilts and pillows and as insulation. If stuffed in boots they provided

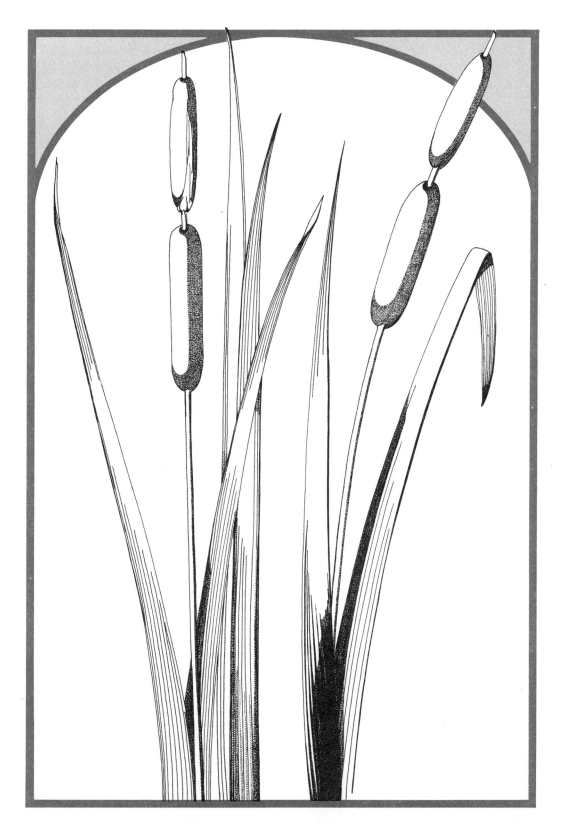

some protection against the cold and possible frostbite.

Cattail leaves were woven into mats and rush seats, and the seed heads were dipped in fat and used as torches. Dusting powder was made by collecting pollen from the male flowers, and the female flowers were used for tinder.

The medicinal and culinary uses of the plant are extensive. North American Indians ate the young shoots like asparagus, and the immature flower spikes were boiled and eaten like corn on the cob. The root was eaten roasted or ground into flour; the pollen was collected and added to bread or cereal.

As medicine the cattail was also useful. The root was often given to women and animals in labor, and when boiled in milk, it was effective against diarrhea. Cattail tea was drunk to help stop hemorrhaging.

The common name comes from the shape of the plant, which could remind one of a cat's tail rising up from the marshes.

COMMON NAME: **celandine**
FAMILY: Papaveraceae (Poppy)
GENUS: *Chelidonium*
SPECIES: *majus*

DESCRIPTION: Celandine's bright yellow flowers have four petals and occur in a loose umbel. The large leaves are pinnately divided and lobed. There is a distinctive bright yellow sap in the stem. The plant grows one to two feet tall.

HABITAT: moist areas, roadsides

BLOOMS: April through August

The genus name *Chelidonium* is from the Greek word for the swallow. Legends and mythology often connect this plant and the swallow, saying that the birds used juice from the stem to strengthen the eyesight of the nestlings. For this reason another common name is swallowwort. Another possibility for this name is that the celandine begins blooming in the spring with the arrival of the swallows and blooms until their departure in the fall.

According to the doctrine of signatures, the yellow sap was used to treat jaundice and liver ailments. The juice was also used to remove warts, corns, and freckles and was used to treat "falling teeth," ringworm,

eczema, and "the itch." It was also thought to be an effective eye medicine. Falconers who had sick birds were said to have used bits of the root to treat them.

Although the plant is attractive growing in the woods, up close it is a rather weedy looking plant. It can grow easily in very poor soil and can get quite aggressive. It has little use as a cut flower, because the leaves and blossoms wilt upon being cut.

An old charm said if you carried celandine with the heart of a mole that you would "vanquish your enemies and win your lawsuits."

COMMON NAME: **cinquefoil**
FAMILY: Rosaceae (Rose)
GENUS: *Potentilla*
SPECIES: *canadensis*

DESCRIPTION: The leaves of this plant are divided into five deeply toothed leaflets. The blossoms occur singly on a stalk, are bright yellow with five petals and several stamens, and look a bit like miniature roses. Some species have white or cream colored flowers. This is a creeping plant that lies close to the ground, growing only two to six inches high.

HABITAT: common, especially in dry, open places

BLOOMS: March through June

———— ✁ ————

The name *Potentilla* is indicative of the powers attributed to cinquefoil over the years, especially during the Middle Ages. It was believed to possess strong medicinal powers and to be quite potent. A tea made from the leaves was used as a gargle and mouthwash and was said to cure inflammation of the mouth and gums. A poultice made from the plant was put on skin wounds.

Witches of earlier ages used cinquefoil as a drug, rubbing it over their bodies to produce a trancelike state. The juice of the plant was mixed with such ingredients as deadly nightshade, hemlock, thorn apple, and spider's legs, and was made into a virulent witch's brew. Curiously enough, in addition to being used by witches, cinquefoil was also used as protection against witches.

Because the plant bears two blossom colors, there arose a superstition that if a

pregnant woman drank a tea made from the white blossoms, she would have a baby girl; drinking a tea made from the yellow blossoms would bring a baby boy.

It has been recorded that the juice of cinquefoil mixed with corn makes a very good fish bait.

Because cinquefoil can grow with few nutrients, it flourishes in poor soil conditions. The plant may be eradicated simply by fertilizing the soil and letting other plants take over.

Cinquefoil is the symbol of the beloved daughter because when it rains the leaves bend over the flower to cover it, as a mother would protect a beloved daughter. It is also called five-fingers and is sometimes confused with wild strawberry.

COMMON NAME: **coreopsis**
FAMILY: Compositae (Daisy)
GENUS: *Coreopsis*

DESCRIPTION: This plant is often confused with black-eyed Susan, but a close look shows jagged edges on the petal tips, which identify it as coreopsis. Most species have eight bright yellow ray flowers with dark seeds in the center and grow to heights of one to two feet.

HABITAT: common in fields and pastures

BLOOMS: June through July

The common name for this tall-growing herb is from two Greek words: *koris*, meaning "bedbug," and *opsis*, meaning "similar to" or "resembles." Each seed has two "horns" and could, with a little imagination, resemble the common bedbug.

Another common name for this plant was tickseed, because some people believed the seeds looked like ticks instead of bedbugs. The early pioneers used this plant in their mattresses to help repel fleas and bedbugs.

Several species of coreopsis are good garden flowers. The bright yellow blossoms are attractive through the summer, and the plant does especially well in dry, sunny areas.

COMMON NAME: dandelion
FAMILY: Compositae (Daisy)
GENUS: *Taraxacum*
SPECIES: *officinale*

DESCRIPTION: A bright yellow head of flowers is at the top of a hollow stem, which arises from a rosette of basal leaves. The blossoms are about one to two inches across and the stems grow from two to eighteen inches tall. The leaves are a dark green and are, in most cases, deeply toothed.

HABITAT: very common in yards and waste places all over North America

BLOOMS: February through June

Almost everyone is familiar with the dandelion. Its name is French, meaning "the tooth of the lion." This name or its equivalent is used in every country where the plant grows and is descriptive of the toothed margins of the leaves. The number of incisions in the leaves is indicative of the amount of sunlight the plant gets. If the plant grows in full sunlight, the leaves will be deeply toothed; if it grows in a shady area, the leaves will be just slightly toothed. The plant will bloom only if it gets sufficient sunlight. The generic name is from Arabic and Persian and means bitter herb. The species name means that it was sold in the market place. "Tramp with the golden head," as the dandelion is sometimes fondly called, is descriptive of the growth patterns of the plant.

Known even to ancient physicians, the dandelion still plays an important part in modern folk medicine. Because it contains high amounts of vitamins A and C, it is used as a general antidote and also for more specific ailments such as rheumatism. An old mountain superstition says if you drink a cup of dandelion tea every morning and every evening, you will never have rheumatism. A Dutch legend is a variation of this, saying that if you eat dandelion salad on Monday and Thursday, you will always stay healthy. An herbal written in 1821 says that the root of the dandelion is good for impetigo, the itch, and several other ailments including "induration of the liver."

A native of Europe, the plant is often cultivated for its culinary uses. The leaves

are gathered in early spring when they are sweetest and then boiled and eaten like spinach or eaten raw in salad. The first frost revives that springtime sweetness of the leaves. A detailed recipe for making dandelion wine is in Eliot Wigginton's book, *Foxfire II*.

The dandelion is abundant because it has several methods of insuring its survival. The root is buried very deep and is therefore impervious to burrowing animals and fire. During the summer the bitter leaves are not grazed. The silken parachutes are actually seeds and are easily dispersed in the wind. Since these seeds do not have to go through a long dormant period before germinating, it takes less time for a dandelion to grow than most other plants.

Because the blowballs, or parachute heads, are irresistible to children all over the world, there are several superstitions about them. Children commonly believe if they can blow off all the seeds in one breath, then a wish will come true. Other superstitions say if you blow on a blowball, the number of seeds left tells what time it is. Yet another superstition says the number of seeds left on a blowball after a child's good hard puff tells how many children that child will have. If you whisper words of love to your favorite person and blow the seeds gently towards him, the seeds will carry your words to your beloved.

The language of the dandelion is "faithful to you," and it is considered a symbol of time and love.

COMMON NAME: **downy false foxglove**
FAMILY: Scrophulariaceae (Snapdragon)
GENUS: *Aureolaria*
SPECIES: *virginica*

DESCRIPTION: This plant is commonly covered with fine down. The lower leaves have one or two lobes, and the upper leaves are almost all entire. The blossoms are yellow, funnel shaped, and about one inch long. They are arranged along the upper portions of the stem on numerous short stalks. The height of the plant varies from one to five feet.

HABITAT: dry woods and clearings

BLOOMS: June through August

The downy false foxglove was named for its similarity to the cultivated foxglove found so often in gardens. Two species of false foxglove are common: A. *virginica* and A. *laevigata*. These two are often put under one genus, *Gerardia*, which was named for John Gerard (1545–1612). Gerard was gardener to a minister of Queen Elizabeth and is best remembered for publishing his extensive *Herball* in 1597. It was one of the first botanical works published in English.

Many species in this genus are somewhat parasitic on the roots of oak trees. Specimens gathered and dried for use in herbariums all turn black and are unusable.

The name foxglove has several possible origins. Some people believed the "little people" or fairies gave the blossoms to foxes to wear as gloves so they would not be caught raiding the chicken coop. Others claimed if you picked foxglove you would offend the fairies—a practical superstition, that probably was started to keep children from picking the plant, which is very poisonous. Another possible origin of the name is fox's glew, an ancient musical instrument. The bell-shaped flower might have reminded some of this instrument, and then the name eventually became foxglove.

COMMON NAME: **evening primrose**
FAMILY: Onagraceae (Evening Primrose)
GENUS: *Oenothera*
SPECIES: *biennis*

DESCRIPTION: An escape plant from the Midwest prairies, the evening primrose forms colonies by means of creeping underground stems. The leaves are lance-shaped with wavy and toothed margins. The flowers are yellow, have four petals, and are borne on the same stem as the leaves. The leaves are usually four to eight inches long and are alternate.

HABITAT: found in dry open places

BLOOMS: June through September

The genus *Oenothera* can be divided into two distinct groups: those that open in the evening and those that open when the sun is out. Identification is sometimes difficult because this plant hybridizes easily. The evening primrose belongs to the first group. They open at dusk, when the scent becomes much stronger. This is to their advantage, since they are pollinated by night-flying moths and insects. Only a few blossoms open each evening, and after they open the petals drop off. If the flower is not pollinated during the night it will stay open a while in the morning to take a chance on a visit from an interested daytime insect. If you see an evening primrose that is still open in the morning, you can be sure that this particular blossom was a real wall flower in the previous night's festivities. If at the end of the blooming season, several seeds have been set already, then the flowers tend to stay open all day.

Most of the flowers that open in the evening are a solid color, without the color contrasts that help insects find the pollen. Color contrasts would be of little use to a night visiting pollinator, navigating in the dark. The heavy, dusky scents characteristic of night-blooming flowers are enough attraction for the moths and insects that pollinate them. Most of the night flowers are very light colored, so they show up well against the night sky, making them easy to find.

During the first year a strong root system develops, making the plant resistant to drought and fire. The roots are edible during the first year and are especially good if collected before the plant has had a chance to bloom. The roots are used in soups and stews, and the leaves can be chopped up and added to salads. White-tailed deer, small rodents, birds, and caterpillars also eat the evening primrose.

The generic name is from Greek, meaning "wine imbibing." It supposedly increased the desire for drink. Other common names include king's cure all, sand lily, and German rampion.

The evening primrose must have been one of the first plants sent from the New World back to Europe, as it was described by European writers as early as 1600.

COMMON NAME: **field mustard**
FAMILY: Cruciferae (Mustard)
GENUS: *Brassica*
SPECIES: *campestris*

DESCRIPTION: As easy to identify when in seed as when in flower, the mustard plant usually grows to heights of three to six feet. In California, under ideal conditions, the plant sometimes grows as high as telephone poles. The blossoms have four yellow petals. The green seed pods are hard to see until the petals fall off. Then they lengthen into long pods and filled with tiny dark seeds. The bottom leaves are covered with hairs, and the top leaves are smooth.

HABITAT: common all over the United States along roadsides and waste places

BLOOMS: June through September

There is some discrepancy as to the scientific name of the Mustard Family; some call it Brassicaceae and others calling it Cruciferae. The name Cruciferae comes from the fact that the four petals characteristic of all species in the family form a cross where they touch. The common name is a corruption of "must"

seeds from the time when Rome occupied Britain and the seeds were soaked in grape juice or must before being used for seasoning. Today the seeds are still used in salads and in barbecue sauces or for seasoning pickles. Prepared mustard can be made from grinding the seeds. The young greens can be eaten and are good when properly prepared, but they must be cooked one half hour or more to make sure that they are tender.

A powder made from the seeds was eaten to improve the appetite and promote digestion. A poultice made from the seed powder mixed with white bread was put on joints swollen with rheumatism. The seeds are favorites of song birds and are often sold in packaged bird seed mixes.

Flowers do not produce the same amount of nectar during all periods of the day, and certain insects know when the flowers produce the most nectar. The peak nectar producing times for field mustard and for dandelions is early in the morning. Chicory's peak period is also in the morning and clover peaks in the early afternoon. Scientists have shown that honey bees have a sense of timing or a biological clock that tells them exactly when to collect honey. Studies have shown that if bees are fed at certain times during the day, they will return to the feeding stations at exactly that time each day, even if there is no food present. This sense of timing enables the honeybee to collect the greatest possible amount of nectar each day, for he knows when the peak nectar-producing periods are for each of the plants he visits.

MCD
© 1983

COMMON NAME: **field sow thistle**
FAMILY: Compositae (Daisy)
GENUS: *Sonchus*
SPECIES: *asper*

DESCRIPTION: The flowers of this species closely resemble those of the dandelion. However, in the sow thistle there are several yellow flower heads on one stalk, and the smooth stem exudes a milky sap. The leaves are prickly toothed and may or may not be deeply toothed. The plant grows to one to six feet.

HABITAT: fields and waste places

BLOOMS: June through October

Sow thistle has been used and eaten by people and animals for hundreds of years. The common name probably comes from the fact that pigs seem to find it particularly delicious. It is a nutritious food source and was used to treat animals for a variety of ailments, including high blood pressure, fevers, and heart disorders. It was fed to pregnant sows to increase their milk supply. The milky sap was also fed to their human counterparts (nursing mothers) to insure a steady supply of milk. (See doctrine of signatures, Glossary.) A mixture of a few of the leaves and wine was said to hasten childbirth. South African settlers used it to wash their faces, to clear their complexions, and to treat external ulcers.

The leaves are bland, but contain high amounts of vitamin C. It was at one time used to treat people suffering from "wheezing and shortness of breath." It was also much sought after for its supposed power of "prolonging virility in gentlemen." The flower seeds turn into lovely parachutes and were used as a replacement for feathers in stuffing pillows and mattresses.

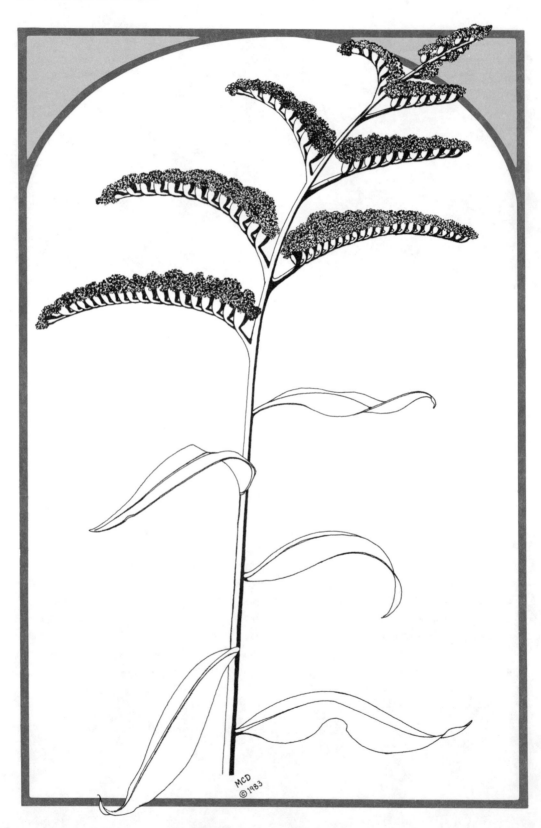

MCD
© 1983

COMMON NAME: **goldenrod**
FAMILY: Compositae (Daisy)
GENUS: *Solidago*

DESCRIPTION: Because there are more than eighty-five species of goldenrods in the United States and many of these interbreed frequently, it is difficult to identify individual species. Most of the species have yellow blossoms (one species has white blossoms), and all bloom in summer and fall. The leaves may be alternate or opposite and are either entire or toothed.

HABITAT: open areas, thickets, along roadsides

BLOOMS: June through November

The goldenrod is truly a North American flower. Only a few species are found growing wild in Mexico, and most of the goldenrods found growing in Europe are cultivated in flower gardens.

Although in the past the blossoms of the goldenrods were dried to make tea, this isn't a good idea because a poisonous fungus often grows on the plants. Nonetheless, during the American Revolution a very popular tea was made from the goldenrod plant.

The goldenrods contain small quantities of rubber, which can be increased with selective hybridization. This has been the subject of extensive research to determine whether it would be economically worthwhile to grow the goldenrod for its rubber content.

The genus name comes from the Latin word that means "to make whole" or "to heal," a name chosen because of medicinal powers the plant was believed to have. American Indians used the goldenrod as a component in steam baths used to steam pain out of an ailing person. A pot of herbs, including goldenrod, was boiled and then set on the floor, and the patient and the pot were covered with a tent of blankets. No steam was allowed to escape until the witch doctor was convinced that all the pain and evil spirits had been forced from the patient's body.

During the reign of Queen Elizabeth,

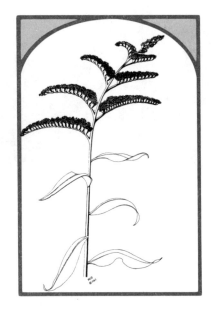

goldenrod powder was exported to London for its healing powers and was sold for as much as a half crown per pound.

One goldenrod superstition says that he who carries the plant will find treasure. Thus, the goldenrod is the symbol for treasure and good fortune.

The following story is told about the origin of goldenrod: An ugly old woman walking in the woods was tired and foot sore. She asked the trees for a walking stick to help her, but all the trees refused her request. However, an old broken stick said to her, "I am old and ugly, but if I can help you please use me." As the old woman emerged from the woods, she turned into a lovely fairy, and turning to the stick, asked what it would like more than anything else in the world. Its answer was simply to be loved by children everywhere. Turning it into a lovely flower and sprinkling gold dust over it, the fairy declared that children all over the world would always love the goldenrod.

This is the state flower of Alabama, Kentucky, and Nebraska.

Common names for the different species describe various physical traits of the plant. Examples are hairy goldenrod, blue-stemmed goldenrod, tall goldenrod, and stiff goldenrod. Seaside goldenrod and Canada goldenrod are named for where they grow, and sweet goldenrod is named for the pleasing scent from the crushed leaves.

COMMON NAME: **goldenseal**
FAMILY: Ranunculaceae (Buttercup)
GENUS: *Hydrastis*
SPECIES: *canadensis*

DESCRIPTION: Numerous yellow-tipped stamens make this plant conspicuous. There are no petals, and the three green sepals drop early. The flowers are solitary, and the leaves are large, thick, and wrinkled. The height of the plant is twelve to fourteen inches.

HABITAT: rich woods

BLOOMS: April through May

There is such a thing as too much of a good thing, and people got so much good out of the goldenseal they nearly caused its extinction. The goldenseal root has been collected for centuries for its medicinal uses. The root is yellow and has been used by American Indians and pioneers as a laxative, a tonic, an astringent, and a stimulant. A salve made from the root was used as an antiseptic for skin sores and to heal external wounds. A powder was used to treat inflammation of the throat and eyes and mouth ulcers. A drug called hydrastine was made from this plant and used to treat malaria.

Also known as yellow Indian paint, the root was used extensively as a natural dye. If the root was mixed with fat, it was useful as an insect repellent. The genus name is from the Greek word for water, *hydro*, and refers to the fact that goldenseal likes water or moist areas. Other common names are orangeroot, eyebalm, Indian turmeric, and ground raspberry.

Goldenseal was at one time used by heroin addicts: when the plant is eaten, certain chemicals mask the presence of heroin or morphine in urine tests. Because of this, new detection tests were devised.

Since it has been collected so extensively, the plant is rare and grows naturally in very few areas. It has bright red fruit, can be propagated by seed in the fall or spring, and prefers a shady area with rich, moist soil.

MCD
© 1983

COMMON NAME: **jewelweed**

FAMILY: Balsaminaceae (Touch-me-not)

GENUS: *Impatiens*

SPECIES: *capensis*

DESCRIPTION: This leafy annual can grow up to five feet tall. It is a succulent plant with bright yellow-orange flowers that hang down from slender, drooping pedicels. There are three petals spotted with brown and three sepals, one of which curls around to form a sac with a long spur. The plant is glaucous and tends to repel water.

HABITAT: wet places, shady areas

BLOOMS: July through frost

The fruits of this plant coil around as they mature and, when disturbed, shoot seeds out great distances. This accounts for the common names, touch-me-not and snapweed. The plant got the common name jewelweed because it repels water, but if water droplets happen to stay on horizontal surfaces, they reflect light and look like jewels. Another possible reason for this name is that the flowers hang down like a jewel on a necklace. Still another common name is lady's ear drops. American Indians called it crowing cock for the shape of the flower.

The sac in the spur of the flower contains a liquid that soothes the rash resulting from poison ivy. American Indians used this juice to treat athlete's foot and other skin ailments. Modern testing has found that this juice contains chemicals that are considered fungicides.

Jewelweed is very easy to grow in a moist, shady spot. It blooms all summer and is a treat for hummingbirds.

COMMON NAME: **yellow lady's slipper**
FAMILY: Orchidaceae (Orchid)
GENUS: *Cypripedium*
SPECIES: *calceolus*

DESCRIPTION: This rather rare plant has a single slender stem that bears one or two flowers. The tip of the flower is yellow, and the sepals are twisted and a brownish or purplish color.

HABITAT: prefers moist, acidic soil

BLOOMS: April through July

The Orchid family is very large, consisting of some 10,000 species. All species are very dependent on insects for pollination and the lady's slipper takes every precaution for being well pollinated. Once the insect, usually a bee, enters the lip of the blossom, it cannot escape the way it came in because the lip is rolled toward the inside. In finding its way out of the lip the bee fills itself with nectar and then escapes by way of a tiny hole designed to scrape the pollen off the bee's back. As it struggles to escape, more pollen gets on its back and goes along to the next plant the bee visits. In this way the lady's slipper is assured of cross pollination.

Because of its inability to adapt to a wide range of environmental conditions, it is difficult to grow in a wildflower garden. In addition, for the plant to be fertilized, a specific type of fungus must be present within the flower. When searching in the woods for the yellow lady's slipper, look in stands of mature pines—the plant prefers an acid soil.

Other common names for the plant include whippoorwill shoes, and Noah's ark. The species name, *calceolus*, is Latin and means "a little shoe."

COMMON NAME: **marsh marigold**
FAMILY: Ranunculaceae (Buttercup)
GENUS: *Caltha*
SPECIES: *palustris*

DESCRIPTION: There are no petals on this plant, but there are five to nine bright yellow petal-like sepals. The leaves are kidney shaped and glossy, and the stem is thick, hollow, and branching, growing to a height of one to two feet.

HABITAT: wet meadows, marshes, swamps

BLOOMS: April through June

Although the marsh marigold is sometimes known as king's cup, it is more often known as cowslip. It is quite different, however, from the Virginia cowslip, which is in the forget-me-not family. The name cowslip is from the Anglo-Saxon word *cuslyppe*, *cu* meaning "cow," and *slyppe* meaning "slop," so clowslip actually means cow slop or cow dung.

The species name is Latin for "of the swamps" and indicates where the plant can be found growing. The name marigold could be from the Anglo-Saxon word *mere*, which means marsh, but more likely it is from the use of the flowers during festivals in medieval times. It was thought that the plant was named in honor of the Virgin Mary.

Although the leaves were cooked and eaten as greens, the raw leaves were thought to be somewhat poisonous. The leaves contain a lot of iron and were used to treat anemia. The flower buds can be boiled or sauteed or even pickled, and the blossoms have been used to make wine. The petals were used extensively in potions and brews during medieval times. Rubbing the leaves on insect bites or bee stings was thought to alleviate pain and itching.

Marsh marigolds were said to bloom so profusely in England that the streams looked yellow.

This species looks more like a buttercup than a marigold. A related species (C. *natans*), known as floating marsh marigold, has pinkish flowers and floating stems.

MCD
© 1983

COMMON NAME: **mullein**
FAMILY: Scrophulariaceae (Snapdragon)
GENUS: *Verbascum*
SPECIES: *thapsus*

DESCRIPTION: One of the easiest plants to identify, the mullein is characterized during the first year of growth by a basal rosette of soft flannel-like leaves. The second year the plant grows to heights of two to six feet or more, and the leaves grow down the sides of the flowering stem. The yellow flowers occur in a terminal spike and are conspicuous because of their orange stamens. The stem is stout and may be branched or not.

HABITAT: roadsides, waste places

BLOOMS: June through November

The variety of common names for this plant—beggar's blanket, flannel plant, Aaron's rod, velvet plant, and witch's candle—suggests how widely it has been used since the time of the Roman Empire.

A native of Europe, mullein was used by Roman soldiers for torches. The stalks dipped in tallow would burn for a fairly long time. The thick down of the plant is still used in parts of Europe as candle wick. Not to be outdone by the men, Roman ladies also found a use for mullein. They used the yellow dye found in the plant to color their hair.

The name witch's candle came from the fact that the plant was considered a potent charm against the demons. It was supposedly used by witches and warlocks in their secret brews. It was believed that those who dealt with the devil would use this plant to light their way, and because of this it was also sometimes called higtaper or hag's taper. Mullein was also used as a love potion.

Quaker rouge was another common name. Quaker ladies, unable to use cosmetics due to their religion, would rub the downy mullein leaves on their cheeks to

make them red. A permanent green dye can be made from the leaves of the mullein by extracting the pigments and then adding sulphuric acid.

Poor peasants and gypsies in Europe found out that lining their shoes with the leaves from this plant gave some protection from the cold. Cattlemen might know the mullein as cow's or bullock's lungwort, because it has been used since ancient times for the treatment of pulmonary congestion in cattle. The seeds, which are protected by an egg shaped capsule, are sometimes eaten during the winter by small birds. Fish that eat the seeds are said to be so sluggish that they can be caught by hand.

American Indians boiled the leaves and applied them to body joints to relieve the aches of rheumatism. Choctaws applied them directly to the head to relieve a headache. The smoked leaves were used for respiratory ailments, and during the early 1900s a cough medicine made from mullein was popular in America. Research has shown that the mullein plant contains chemicals that are useful in softening the skin or soothing inflamed tissue.

The name mullein comes from the Latin word *mollis*, which means soft. The species name honors Thapsus, an ancient town in Africa in what is now Tunisia. The generic name, *Verbascum*, is a corruption of the Latin *barbascum*, meaning "with beard."

COMMON NAME: **oxalis**
FAMILY: Oxalidaceae (Wood Sorrel)
GENUS: *Oxalis*
SPECIES: *stricta*

DESCRIPTION: The stems arise from slender rhizoids and are covered with small white hairs. The leaves are clover shaped, and there are usually three to a stem. There are two to seven yellow flowers on a plant. The height of the plant is three to six inches.

HABITAT: common in woods, waste places, and cities, where it is found so often it is considered a cosmopolitan weed.

BLOOMS: May through frost

Oxalis is one of the most popular woodland treats. The stalks and leaves may be chewed directly or added to a lettuce salad. All species, however, have a sour watery juice containing oxalic acid, which is poisonous if consumed in large quantities—so don't eat too much. The word oxalis means sour.

The leaves are sensitive to the cold and close up at night as protection from the change in temperatures, which gives it the name sleeping beauty.

The white oxalis is often referred to as alleluia flower because it blooms during the Easter season. Because of this the oxalis is the symbol of joy. Other names for this plant include sour trefoil, bread and cheese, and yellow wood-sorrel.

Oxalis is pollinated by syphus flies, small bees, or small butterflies. Self-pollination is also possible. The plant is hard to get out of a garden once it gets a good start, because the underground runners are very tough.

COMMON NAME: **Indian strawberry**
FAMILY: Rosaceae (Rose)
GENUS: *Duchesnea*
SPECIES: *indica*

DESCRIPTION: The coarsely toothed leaflets of this plant are dark green and occur in threes. The stems propagate by runners and often cover a wide area. The blossoms have five yellow petals, and the red fruit averages about three-fourths inch across. The flower stem may grow three inches tall.

HABITAT: very common in dry woods and roadsides

BLOOMS: April through June

The name strawberry was given by the peasants who laid straw around the plants to keep them from being spoiled during wet weather. The generic name is from N. Duchesne, a world authority on strawberries who worked on hybridizing and improving the cultivated strains to find the most delicious berries. Yet the Indian strawberry is tasteless. The species name is from the original home of this plant, India.

American Indians crushed the berries and made one of the first facial masks for improving the complexion. They also put the roots in boiling water to make a tea that was used to cure diarrhea and stomach cramps. Birds, turtles, small rodents, and bears eat the berries.

It is easy to confuse this plant with the true wild strawberry, which has delicious fruit, when they are not in bloom. True wild strawberry can be distinguished by its white blossoms, in contrast to the yellow blossoms of Indian strawberry.

COMMON NAME: **sunflower**
FAMILY: Compositae (Daisy)
GENUS: *Helianthus*
SPECIES: *annus*

DESCRIPTION: Sunflowers are most often found in the Midwest in the prairie areas. The blossoms are easy to identify: the ray flowers are bright yellow, and the disk flowers are a reddish brown. The leaves are heart-shaped and alternate, the stem slender. It can grow to a height of three to ten feet.

HABITAT: prairies, wasteplaces, and roadsides

BLOOMS: July through September

The common name is translated directly from the genus name, which is made up of two Greek words: *helios*, "sun", and *anthos*, "flower."

During the nineteenth century, American settlers planted sunflowers near their homes as protection against malaria. The leaves and stalks were used for fodder. Fibers from the stalks were used to make cloth, and the leaves were dried and smoked like tobacco. The young sprouts and the seeds were eaten, the seed husks were ground and made into a coffeelike drink, and oil from the seeds was used in cooking and making soap. A permanent yellow dye was made from the ray flowers of the blossom.

Probably due to the lofty heights the sunflower can grow to, the language of the plant is haughtiness.

The Inca Indians of Peru worshipped the sunflower as a symbol of the sun. The priestesses in the temple of the sun wore necklaces of sunflowers made from gold. Spanish explorers in Peru took sunflower seeds back to Spain with them. There they were cultivated and hybridized and, centuries later, were reintroduced as cultivated plants in America.

North American Indians were found cultivating sunflowers along the shores of Lake Huron. In cultivation, the plants can grow as high as twenty feet. The Indians used ground seeds for flour and oil from the seeds for cooking, mixing paints, and dressing their hair.

Sunflowers are easy to grow in a wildflower garden, but must have full sun to bloom. They can be grown in a border or mixed with cultivated plants.

This is the state flower of Kansas.

COMMON NAME: **tansy**
FAMILY: Compositae (Daisy)
GENUS: *Tanacetum*
SPECIES: *vulgare*

DESCRIPTION: The bright yellow buttonlike flowers look like a daisy without its white petals. The flower heads are composed almost entirely of disk flowers. The leaves are finely dissected, fernlike, and aromatic. The plant grows to a height of two to three feet.

HABITAT: roadsides and waste places

BLOOMS: July through September

Tansy tea has been used since the Middle Ages to treat a variety of ailments, none of which could be as bad as tansy tea itself. The leaves have a strong, bitter taste, and tea made from them has a vile and bitter taste. This tea was used to cure rheumatism and intestinal worms; was put on the skin to help boils, pimples, and sunburn; was thought to "bring out" measles and promote menstruation, and was used for hundreds of years as an abortive. A similar species, *Tanacetum parthenium*, was slightly analgesic and was used as a sixteenth-century pain killer.

To put a leaf on the navel of a pregnant woman was thought to induce childbirth. A powder made from the leaves was used to kill fleas and lice. The young leaves and flowers were used in cooking as a substitute for sage.

The bitter juice from the tansy was used during the fifteenth century in paschal cakes. These cakes are a reminder of the bitter herbs eaten by the Jews at Passover.

The genus name and the common name both have roots from the Greek word *athanasia*, a medicine to prolong life. The scent from the plant is long lasting, and it

MCD
©1983

became customary to place the leaves inside coffins or to rub the bodies of the dead with the leaves. This was thought to preserve the body.

Other common names are bitterbuttons, scented fern, and stinking Willie.

The language of tansy is "I declare war against you."

COMMON NAME: **trout lily**
FAMILY: Liliaceae (Lily)
GENUS: *Erythronium*
SPECIES: *americanum*

DESCRIPTION: The leaves of this perennial are large and basal with conspicuous spots. The sepals are yellow and are reflexed back, often showing brown or reddish coloring underneath. It grows to heights of four to ten inches.

HABITAT: common in rich woods and meadows

BLOOMS: February through May

The lily is the sacred flower of motherhood. It is the symbol for many goddesses, including the Greek goddess Hera, who was responsible for a woman's marriage and childbirth, and for the Roman goddess Juno, who was responsible for the lives of women.

The Christian legend is that the lily sprang from Eve's tears when she found she was approaching motherhood. Another legend says the white lily, or the Easter lily, was not white until it was picked by the Virgin Mary. The lily is the Christian symbol of purity, chastity, innocence, the Resurrection and Easter.

The trout lily got its name from the fact that the leaves are spotted, resembling a trout. Also, it blooms during trout season.

Other common names are fawn lily, because of the two leaves that stand straight up like the ears of a fawn, and adder's tongue, from the long, protruding stamens. The white bulb that this plant grows from is responsible for the name dogtooth violet, although it is not a true violet. The generic name comes from a Greek word that means "red" and refers to the reddish brown spots on the leaves.

The leaves are edible and can be cooked and eaten with butter as a vegetable. The bulbs were often stored in root cellars to be used as winter food. Black and grizzly bears eat the bulbs, and deer eat the green seed pods.

Trout lily tea was supposedly a cure for the hiccups. Roman soldiers grew it near

MCD
© 1983

their camps and used it on foot sores and corns.

The Roman philosopher Pliny recorded a recipe for getting purple blossoms from the lily plants. He suggested that one soak the bulbs of the plant in a red wine until they turned a red color.

COMMON NAME: **whorled loosestrife**
FAMILY: Primulaceae (Primrose)
GENUS: *Lysimachia*
SPECIES: *quadrifolia*

DESCRIPTION: The starlike flowers have pointed yellow petals and a reddish center. The blossoms are borne on narrow stalks from the axils of the leaves, which are light green and occur in whorls of three to six. The height of the plant is one to three feet.

HABITAT: old fields, clearings, open woods

BLOOMS: June through August

Both the common and the generic names of this plant refer to the supposed power of the plant to soothe animals or "loose them from their strife." Legend tells us that King Lysimachus of Sicily was walking through a field when a bull began to chase him. The good king grabbed this plant and waved it in front of the bull, calming him, and loosing him from his strife. It was thought that tying a branch of the plant to the yoke of oxen would make them easier to handle. It was also found that the plant helped to repel gnats and other irritating insects, and perhaps this explains why the animals were easier to handle with loosestrife close by. Pliny wrote that the very odor of loosestrife would keep snakes away.

The juice from the flowers was used to dye hair blond. The crushed leaves were used to heal sores caused by too tight boots or shoes.

A similar species, *nummularia*, is called moneywort because the leaves look like small coins. In the 1500s it was known as "herba two pence."

COMMON NAME: **yellow star grass**
FAMILY: Amaryllidaceae (Amaryllis)
GENUS: *Hypoxis*
SPECIES: *hirsuta*

DESCRIPTION: Until it is in bloom, this plant can easily be mistaken for one of the grasses, as the foliage is long and slender. The flower is bright yellow and consists of three petals and three sepals, all of which are the same size and color. There are six stamens and one pistil. One or two flowers can usually be found at the top of the stem, which is shorter than the surrounding foliage, growing only ten to twelve inches tall.

HABITAT: common in dry woods and meadows

BLOOMS: April through August

Both the genus and species names are descriptive of this plant. *Hypoxis* is made up of two Greek words, which mean "sharp beneath" and refer to the sharp, black seeds.

Hirsuta means "hairy" and refers to the downy stem and undersides of the sepals and petals. The plant is also known as hairy stargrass.

PINK FLOWERS

COMMON NAME: hedge bindweed
FAMILY: Convolvulaceae (Morning Glory)
GENUS: *Convolvulus*
SPECIES: *sepium*

DESCRIPTION: The funnel-shaped morning-glory kind of flower has two heart-shaped bracts growing under the blossom. These bracts are absent in the cultivated morning glory. The flower is pink with white stripes and the leaves are arrow-shaped.

HABITAT: fields and thickets

BLOOMS: May through September

The growth habits of this plant have earned it a number of common names. The twisting and turning stem that will encircle anything in its path in a surprisingly short time has been responsible for names like bindweed and bearbind (suggesting, perhaps, that if a bear stood still long enough, even it could be entwined). The profusion of circular stems and tendrils probably inspired the names old man's nightcap, devil's guts, and hedge-bell. It closely resembles the cultivated morning glory, so it is often called wild morning glory. The genus name also refers to the growth pattern: *Convolvulus* is from the Latin word *convolvo*, which means "to entwine." The species name, *sepium*, is also from Latin and means "of hedges or fences," describing where the species is most often found growing. A closely related species, *Convolvulus arvensis*, grows in waste places and fields and is also appropriately named, as *arvensis* is Latin, meaning "of cultivated fields."

Whatever bindweed is called, though, it is an extremely hardy and aggressive plant. It seems to flourish in any type of soil. Hand weeding seems to be the most effective way to get rid of the plant, although it has been suggested that if you unwind the main stem and rewind it in the opposite direction, the plant will die.

A tea made by dropping a handful of leaves into boiling water was drunk a quarter of an hour before breakfast as a gentle laxative. Women drank this tea to help stomach cramps or to guard against a miscarriage. The fresh leaves, made into a poultice, helped to bring a boil to a head. American Indians were said to have rubbed the leaves of the plant over their bodies and then handled rattlesnakes without danger.

An extract from bindweed was once used as flavoring in a liqueur.

Bindweed was also part of witch lore. The witches were said to wrap the plant nine times around a figure representing a victim. The spell was especially effective when used three days before a full moon.

The language of the bindweed is humility.

COMMON NAME: **fireweed**
FAMILY: Onagraceae (Evening Primrose)
GENUS: *Epilobium*
SPECIES: *angustifolium*

DESCRIPTION: The tall stem (two to six feet) is generally unbranched and holds numerous large pink or purple flowers, with the lower flowers blooming first. The leaves are entire and lance-shaped, alternate and numerous.

HABITAT: open areas, especially recently burned areas

BLOOMS: July through September

This plant, which grows throughout the northern regions of the world, is most noticeable in places that have recently been burned. Areas devastated by forest fires soon turn pinkish purple from the blossoms of fireweed. After London was bombed during World War II, acres and acres of the plant could be seen. One reason fireweed prospers in such areas is that it cannot tolerate shade and, of course, there is no shade in burned areas.

Fireweed has an excellent reproductive system, with creeping stems in addition to easily dispersed seeds.

Fireweed honey made by bees feeding on the fireweed plant is much prized by honey connoisseurs.

The leaves of the plant were dried and added to other tea leaves to make an unusual, tasty tea. The young shoots were boiled and eaten like asparagus. Parts of the

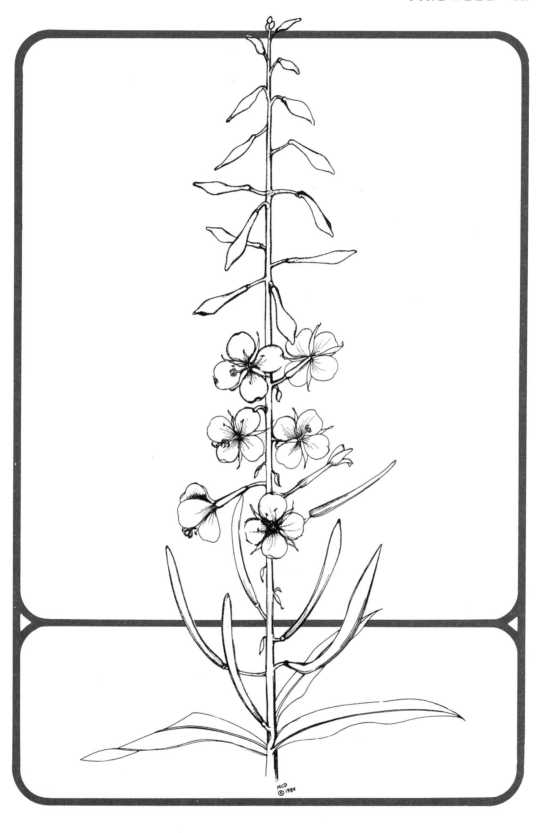

McD
© 1984

plant were at one time used to treat asthma and whooping cough.

The name *Epilobium* is Greek ("upon the pod") and refers to the blooming pattern the plant exhibits. The blossoms open successively going up the stem, the lower flowers opening first. Because of this there can be seed pods on the lower portions of the stalk, open blossoms on the middle sections, and buds at the top. The species name means "narrow leafed." Other common names refer to the shape of the leaf, which is similar to those of the willow tree: great willow-herb and willowweed. It has also been called blooming Sally. The lovely color of the blossoms has been referred to as Oriental purple.

COMMON NAME: **wild geranium**
FAMILY: Geraniaceae (Geranium)
GENUS: *Geranium*
SPECIES: *maculatum*

DESCRIPTION: The stem is hairy and grows one to two feet tall. The leaves occur in pairs and are deeply five-parted, and sharply toothed, usually measuring four to five inches across. The flowers have five pink or purplish petals and ten stamens. As the leaves get older, they are often spotted with white.

HABITAT: common in woodlands and open areas or shady roadsides

BLOOMS: April through June

Both the common and scientific names of this plant are based on the fact that the fruit resembles a crane's beak. The word Geranium is Greek for crane, and one of the more commonly used names is crane's bill. The species name means spotted and is descriptive of the leaves as they get older. Other common names include shameface (for the color of the flower), alum root, and rock weed, since it often grows on rocky slopes.

Legend says that geraniums were descendants of the mallow. The story goes that once the prophet Mohammed washed his shirt in a stream and laid it on a bed of mallow to dry. The flowers blushed deep pink at their distinction and have been called the geraniums ever since.

Although pollination by insects is widely understood now, man did not always know how insects and plants help each other out. It was the geranium that first brought man's

attention to the relationship between plants and insects. Self-pollination in the plant is impossible, since the pistils mature after the stamens do. Because surrounding plants are at various stages of maturity, it is entirely pollinated by insects, usually honeybees.

The wild geranium was much treasured for its medicinal values. A concoction made from the boiled root was used in the treatment of sore throats and mouth ulcers. A tea brewed from the leaves was a treatment for dysentery. American Indians used it as a tonic and as an astringent. Northern Indian tribes used the powdered root when they were wounded to help the blood coagulate. This was effective due to the tannin content in the roots. It has also been used to help prevent hemorrhages.

The language of the geranium is constancy and availability. Send it to your lover, and it says "I desire to please." The popular potted plant is in the same family, but of a different species.

COMMON NAME: showy lady's slipper
FAMILY: Orchidaceae (Orchid)
GENUS: *Cypripedium*
SPECIES: *reginae*

DESCRIPTION: The flowers of the Orchid Family are characterized by having three petals that are very similar and one petal that is quite different. The three similar petals of this species are lateral, white, flat, and long. The slipper, or dissimilar petal, is pink or reddish, or rarely, white. The plant grows to a height of one to three feet. The leaves are oval, strongly ribbed, and clasp the stem.

HABITAT: wet woods, swampy places, or bogs

BLOOMS: June through July

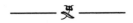

Because it is somewhat rare, finding the showy lady's slipper is quite a treat. Even if it were abundant, seeing the flower would still be a delight because of its exquisite beauty. Insects also find the plant exciting and flock around it when it is in bloom.

The lady's slipper helps insects to find the pollen by having pathways marked all over the blossom: the pink veins in the petals

lead the insects to the one spot they can enter to find the nectar.

The hairs covering the stem protect the plant from being eaten—they contain a fatty acid that is poisonous to many animals and to people. The reaction is similar to that from poison ivy.

Both the common and scientific names refer to the slipper-shaped lower petal. The generic name is from Greek and translates as "Venus' slipper."

Although beautiful in a wildflower garden, the plants are subject to fungus blight and are difficult to keep alive. The blight is easily detected, as there are usually spots on the leaves. The lady's slipper grows best at a soil pH of about 4.0.

This is the state flower of Minnesota.

COMMON NAME: **marsh mallow**
FAMILY: Malvaceae (Mallow)
GENUS: *Althaea*
SPECIES: *officinalis*

DESCRIPTION: There are five pink petals, numerous stamens, and a single pistil. Several blossoms cluster in the leaf axils. The leaves are grey-green, soft, toothed, and heart shaped.

HABITAT: along the coast and in marshy areas

BLOOMS: August through October

Yes, marshmallows did come from the marsh mallow, and the plants were once cultivated for this purpose. The roots contain a gelatinous substance that was used to make cough syrups as well as marshmallows. The root, which looks like a thin yellow carrot, was once used as a baby "teether." The hard root softened as the baby chewed and released mucilage, which was thought to have a calming effect on the baby's stomach.

The name mallow is from the Greek word *malakos*, which means "soft" and refers to the leaves. The genus name is Greek ("that which heals") and indicates that this plant at one time had extensive medicinal usage. Pliny suggested that one tablespoon of the mallows daily would keep you free of disease. Among the specific ailments mallow was supposed to cure were cramps and convulsions, bee stings, dandruff and loss of hair, coughs, sore throats and swollen glands, inflammation and swelling of breasts, and

"sharp fretting humours." The water in which the plant was boiled was used to soften chapped skin.

A woodland substitute for meringue or whipped cream was to cover the fruits of the marsh mallows with water and boil until the liquid was reduced by half. The resulting liquid was then cooled and whipped until frothy.

The French word for mallow is mauve, which is descriptive of one of the colors the mallow can be.

COMMON NAME: **phlox**
FAMILY: Polemoniaceae (Phlox)
GENUS: *Phlox*
SPECIES: *carolina*

DESCRIPTION: Often growing to a height of three feet or more, this is one of the taller species of phlox. The phlox hybridize in the wild easily and therefore are sometimes difficult to identify. The leaves of this species are two to four inches long with smooth margins. The flower heads are a terminal cylinder of deep pink to purplish blossoms.

HABITAT: common in dry woods or open places

BLOOMS: May through October

Although the phlox is extensively cultivated, several species have "escaped" and grow wild. More than forty species of phlox grow in the United States.

The word phlox is Greek, meaning flame, and describes the color of the flower. The language of the flower is sweet dreams and a proposal of love.

Phlox leaves were often crushed and added to water to cure such ailments as an upset stomach, sore eyes, and skin diseases.

An extract made from the leaves was used as a laxative.

The phloxes were original Americans and were exported to Europe where they were easily grown in rock and ornamental gardens. It was not cultivated in North America until it was reintroduced through European horticulturists. Probably the greatest single virtue of the phlox is its sweet scent, which is especially strong in the early evening.

MCD
© 1983

COMMON NAME: **spring beauty**
FAMILY: Portulacaceae (Purslane)
GENUS: *Claytonia*
SPECIES: *virginica*

DESCRIPTION: Spring beauty stems arise from a deep tuber and are six to twelve inches tall. The two leaves are opposite one another and are grasslike, being much taller than they are wide. There can be as many as fifteen flowers from the same tuber. The flowers are white with deep pink veins or all pink. The lower flowers on the stem open first, and as the season progresses, flowers farther up the stem will open.

HABITAT: common in moist rich woods

BLOOMS: March through May

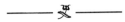

Because it is one of the earliest flowers to bloom in the spring, the delicate spring beauty has a special place in the hearts of flower lovers everywhere. It is the epitome of the spring flower: delicate, sweet smelling, and beautiful. It does very well in a wildflower garden, since it is easy to transplant and just as easy to grow.

Not only humans look forward to the blooming of the spring beauty—the flowers and leaves are eaten by elk, moose, deer, and sheep. The roots are edible as well and are tasty. Raw, they have the sharp taste of radishes, and when boiled or baked, they have the taste and texture of baked potatoes. One enthusiast described the taste as being between a very good baked potato and roasted chestnuts.

The generic name, *Claytonia*, is from John Clayton, who was an early American botanist and physician.

Spring beauty is of special interest to geneticists, because unlike almost every other living organism, the plant has an unstable number of chromosomes. Whereas all humans have forty-six chromosomes, the number of chromosomes present in each individual spring beauty plant varies. There are fifty possible chromosomal combinations in this plant.

Although most species of this genus are found in North America, five species grow in the Arctic.

This plant is most often pollinated by bees and small butterflies, but as many as seventy-one species of insects have been recorded pollinating the spring beauty.

A closely related species, C. *caroliniana*, grows frequently in the moist, rich woods of the mountains.

ORANGE&RED FLOWERS

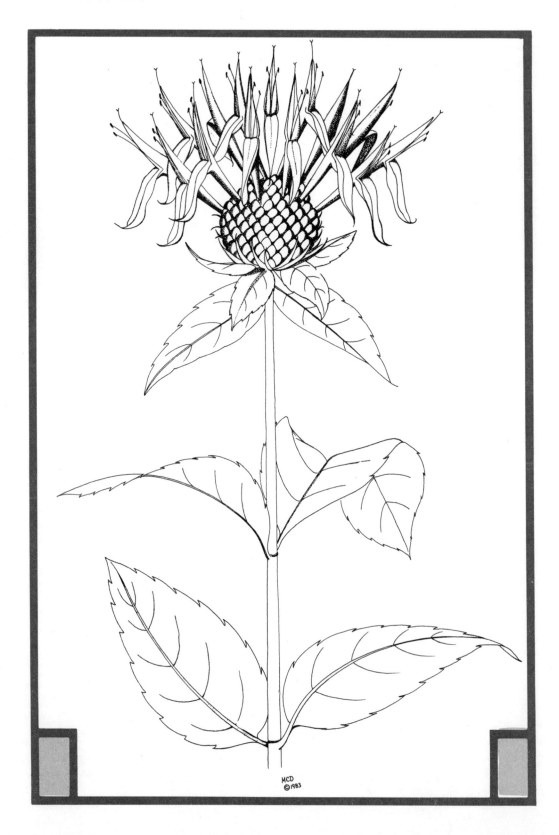

MCD
©1983

COMMON NAME: **beebalm**
FAMILY: Labiatae (Mint)
GENUS: *Monarda*
SPECIES: *didyma*

DESCRIPTION: This showy plant has a rounded terminal head of bright red tubular flowers. Reddish brown bracts are numerous. The stem is square and the leaves paired and opposite, as is characteristic of the Mint Family.

HABITAT: prefers moist places, rich woods, and streambanks

BLOOMS: June through August

The name beebalm might suggest that this flower is pollinated by bees, but just the opposite is true. The red flowers and tubular arrangement of the blossoms make it particularly attractive to hummingbirds, and it can be pollinated by butterflies. Pollination by bees, however, is virtually impossible because of the shape of the blossom and the relatively heavy weight of the bee.

Another frequently used common name, Oswego tea, is more legitimate. John Bartram, during his extensive travels in North America, visited an outpost on Lake Ontario in the center of Oswego Indian country. The settlers in this area used the leaves of beebalm and made a very tasty mint-like tea. This was especially popular during the Revolutionary War. John Bartram was impressed with the plant because of the combination of fragrant leaves and colorful blossoms.

Other common names include Indian plume, fragrant balm, and mountain mint. The genus name is from Nicholas Monardes (1493-1588), a Spanish botanist who took particular interest in plants found in the New World. The species name, *didyma*, is from a Greek word meaning "paired" or "twinned" and refers to the two stamens found in each flower.

Beebalm's strong mint flavor made it useful for flavoring in cooking. It was also found to be soothing for stomach aches and for cooling fevers. Perhaps the plant was also used to soothe bee or insect stings and this is the reason for the name beebalm.

Beebalm is nice for a wildflower garden because it blooms all summer and the flowers are such a lovely color. Josephine W. Johnson in *The Inland Island* described the color of beebalm as being "a peculiar red, neither crimson nor luminous. A wood red."

It prefers moist, slightly acid soil and can be propagated by division in the spring, cuttings in late summer, or seeds sown nearly anytime.

COMMON NAME: **butter-and-eggs**
FAMILY: Scrophulariaceae (Snapdragon)
GENUS: *Linaria*
SPECIES: *vulgaris*

DESCRIPTION: The flowers are only one inch long and have five petals: three lower ones that are orange colored and have a spur at the base, and two upper ones that are yellow and erect. The upper leaves are alternate and grasslike and the lower ones are opposite and whorled.

HABITAT: roadsides, dry fields

BLOOMS: May through October

Butter-and-eggs is a prevalent summer plant. Mary Durant, in her book *Who Named the Daisy? Who Named the Rose?* described it as being a "common, handsome, tedious weed" and "showy, but very obnoxious." The common name butter-and-eggs is from the two colors found in the flower, yellow (the butter) and orange (the eggs). Another common name given to this plant is ranstead or ramstead, for it was supposedly brought to America by a gentleman from Wales, a Mr. Ramstead. It is also called dead-men's-bones and gallwort, the latter because it was fed to chickens to rid them of gall stones. The genus name is based on the Latin word for flax, *linum*, because the leaves look somewhat like those of flax. This is also why it is simetimes called toadflax. The "toad" part is because the flower opens its mouth like a toad when it is squeezed a certain way. The species name, *vulgaris*, is from the Latin word for "common" and refers to the prevalence of the plant.

The very scent of butter-and-eggs makes one believe in its medicinal powers. It smells cheesy or slightly sweet or even medicinal. Tea made from the leaves was used for constipation and to treat jaundice and conjunctivitis. Made into a salve, it soothed insect bites. It was brought from Europe and

cultivated to use in skin lotions. The juice mixed with milk was used as a fly poison. According to the doctrine of signatures, butter-and-eggs, and all members of the Snapdragon family, were used for treating throat ailments. This was based on the "mouth and throat" arrangement of the blossoms.

This plant's yellow and orange colors made it especially attractive as a dye. They also make it easy for insects to find the nectar and pollinate the flower. This color code of the contrasting colors is so strong that moths will press their tongues on glass between them and the blossom, going for the orange parts every time.

A Scottish superstition said that if you walked around a butter-and-eggs plant three times, any spell would be broken. According to an English superstition, putting three seeds from the plant on a linen thread would protect against all evil.

COMMON NAME: **butterfly-weed**
FAMILY: Asclepiadaceae (Milkweed)
GENUS: *Asclepias*
SPECIES: *tuberosa*

DESCRIPTION: The bright orange blossoms of this flower make it easy to identify. It is one of the most brilliant and beautiful flowers found along the roadsides. The stem is rather rough and hairy, branching often towards the top. The lance-shaped leaves are numerous and are about six inches long. The plant grows to heights of one to two and a half feet.

HABITAT: common in fields and dry soil

BLOOMS: June through September

———— ✻ ————

Unlike most members of the Asclepiadaceae, or Milkweed Family, butterfly-weed has a non-milky sap. Early pioneers believed the root would cure pleurisy, and because of this the plant is sometimes known as pleurisy root. The Indians used the roots in several types of medicine, but today none of them is thought to be effective.

The soft downy seeds were sometimes used as stuffing instead of feathers in beds and cushions. When these seeds were attached by the ends to a woven fabric, it

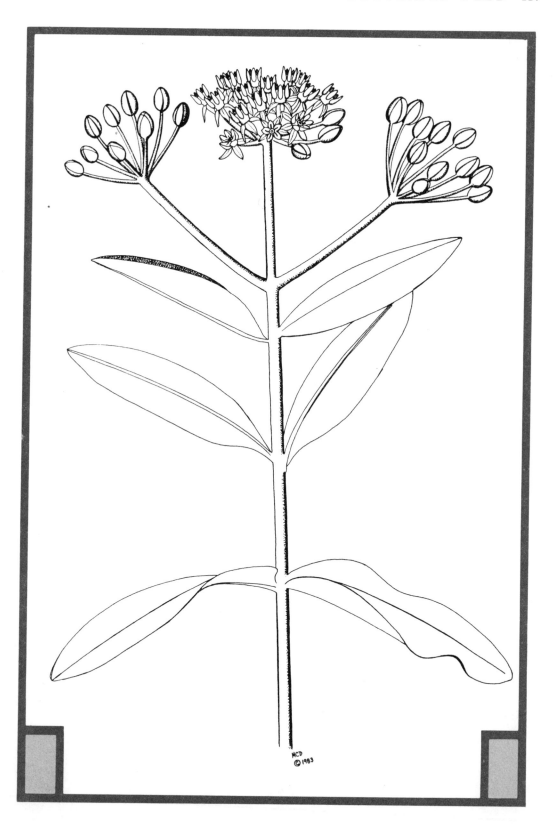

MCD
© 1983

looked like soft, fine fur. They were also used instead of feathers in making hats.

The butterfly-weed adds brilliant color to a wild-flower garden and is relatively easy to transplant and maintain. The younger the plants, the better chance they have of surviving transplanting. The plants do well under a variety of conditions and will thrive even in poor soil if allowed to develop a healthy root system. In addition to making a splash of color in your garden, butterfly-weed will attract several kinds of butterflies. If the blossoms are cut, the plant will bloom at least once more that season.

Another common name, chiggerweed, has prejudiced many people against this plant. This prejudice is unfounded, however, since the butterfly-weed has no more chiggers than most other kinds of weeds.

COMMON NAME: **cardinal flower**
FAMILY: Lobeliaceae (Bluebell)
GENUS: *Lobelia*
SPECIES: *cardinalis*

DESCRIPTION: A spike of brilliant red flowers at the end of a drab green stem makes this plant hard to miss. The numerous leaves are lance shaped, toothed, and alternate. The stem is unbranched and grows to a height of two to four feet. If broken open the stem exudes a milky sap.

HABITAT: common in moist or wet areas

BLOOMS: July through frost

———— ✻ ————

The cardinal flower is typical of flowers pollinated by hummingbirds. It is brightly colored and scentless. Bumblebees have trouble clinging to the blossom, for the lower lip is split and weak. The hummingbirds find this no obstacle, however, for they hover in the air as they collect nectar—and pollinate the flower in the process.

Cardinal flower is a native of North America, and more than thirty species are found in the United States. One of the first plants sent to Europe, it has been cultivated there since the early 1600s. The language of the cardinal flower is distinction and splendor or social affection.

The root of this plant was thought to be a potent love charm. After it was taken out

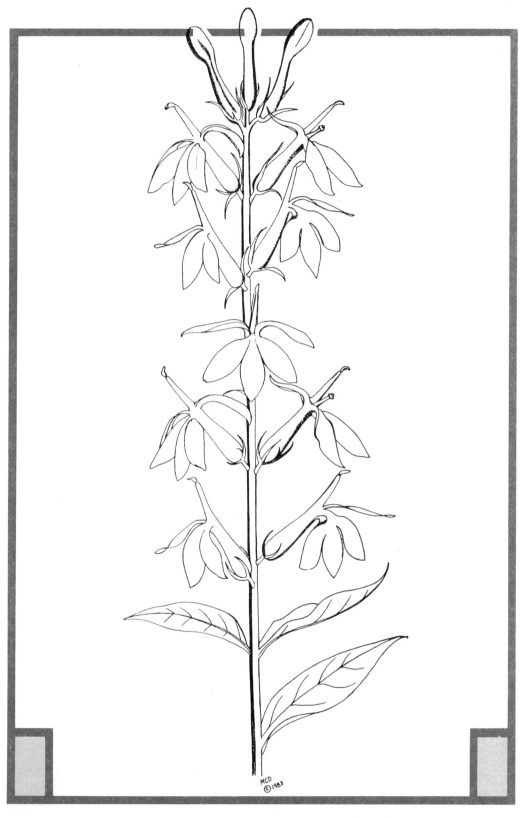

MCD
©1983

of the ground with much ceremony, the root was washed thoroughly and then touched to each part of a person's body. Although the charm was reported to work for people of all ages, it was supposed to be especially effective for elderly ladies.

Indians had a more mundane use for the root. They boiled it and made a tea to cure intestinal worms. Caution should be taken in trying this cure, however, since if it is taken in great quantities it will cause dizziness, sweaty palms, irregular pulse, and nausea.

The scientific name is from a French botanist, Mathis de Lobel. The common name comes from the scarlet-colored blossoms, the same color worn by a cardinal of the Roman Catholic Church. One story says this native American plant was sent to Queen Henrietta Maria of France from one of her colonies. Upon seeing the plant, she giggled and said it reminded her of the red stockings the Catholic cardinals wore. The songbird cardinal was also named for the scarlet robes worn in the Catholic church.

COMMON NAME: **columbine**
FAMILY: Ranunculaceae (Buttercup)
GENUS: *Aquilegia*
SPECIES: *canadensis*

DESCRIPTION: The flowers, which are red and yellow in this species, are made up of five long spurs on a very long slender stem. These flowers are often as much as two inches long, and the stems grow to heights of one foot or more. The flowers hang down from these stems, the spurs pointing upwards. The leaves are divided several times.

HABITAT: Often found on steep slopes, the columbine prefers a dry and open environment.

BLOOMS: March through August

Because the columbine is a symbol of cuckoldry and a deserted lover, it was an insult to give it to a woman and bad luck to give it to a man. The language of the red

flower is anxiety and trembling and that of the blue is resolved to win.

The unusual shape of the flowers lends itself to a number of different common

MCD
©1983

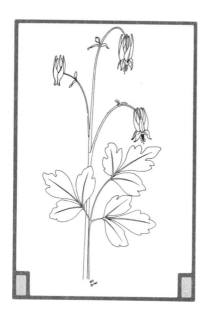

names. It is often incorrectly called honeysuckle, although it has only a slight resemblance to the real honeysuckle. A more descriptive name for it is meeting house, which alludes to the "heads in a circle" that the spurs suggest. The genus name is from the Latin word for eagle; the spurs suggest an eagle's claws. The name columbine is also from the Latin and means "dove," for to some people the spurs look like dove heads in a circle. Rock bells is another name given to it because of the shape of the flower and its natural habitat.

The entire plant was used by ancient herbalists to treat a variety of ailments. The juice of the fresh plant was used to cure jaundice or abdominal pains or to reduce swelling of the liver. A picture of columbine was found on the border of a hand-written manuscript that was dated in the late fifteenth century. The plant was supposedly a cure of measles and smallpox. Columbine contains prussic acid and may have a narcotic effect on some people. An old legend said that lions ate columbine in the spring to gain extra strength.

Although in 1899 the Colorado state legislature declared the white and lavender columbine the state flower, this did not please the school children and in 1911 when the question of the state flower again arose, the school children were the only ones allowed to vote. The blue columbine won an overwhelming victory and is now considered the Colorado state flower. At one time a committee was formed to make the columbine the national flower. The name is similar to the District of Columbia and includes the Latin word for eagle, which is the national bird. The group raised little interest or support, and the matter was dropped.

Columbine is a good plant to grow in a shady area of your yard. Although seeds can be bought, the tiny seedlings are often hard to protect from the weather and established plants are much easier to grow.

MCD
© 1983

COMMON NAME: **fire pink**
FAMILY: Caryophyllaceae (Pink)
GENUS: *Silene*
SPECIES: *virginica*

DESCRIPTION: Bright red flowers with five deeply notched petals and ten stamens are borne in a loose cluster atop a very slender stem. The leaves are lanceolate, entire, and opposite. The plant grows to a height of six to twenty-four inches.

HABITAT: open woods, rocky slopes

BLOOMS: April through June

Catchfly is a common name often associated with members of the Pink (Caryophyllaceae) Family. This name was given because of the sticky sap that exudes from the stem. This sap prevents crawling insects from stealing the nectar without pollinating the flower.

The generic name also refers to this sap, though there are two differing opinions as to the origin of the name. One opinion is that *Silene* is from the Greek word *sialon*, which means "saliva." The other opinion is that the genus name is from Silenus, who was the foster father of Bacchus in Greek mythology. Silenus was often found intoxicated with beer all over his face. The secretions of the catchflies reminded one of this foam and so the plant was named for this character.

Members of this genus were called *gillofloures* in Elizabethan England, and concoctions made from the plants mixed with sugar and wine were thought to be soothing to the heart. The root was also used as a worm medicine.

The star-shaped red flowers are truly outstanding and made a lovely splash of color in a garden. They are relatively easy to transplant. Although it is difficult to get all of the root system, it doesn't seem to harm the plant to leave a few roots behind. It prefers a dry, sandy, open area in a slightly acid soil.

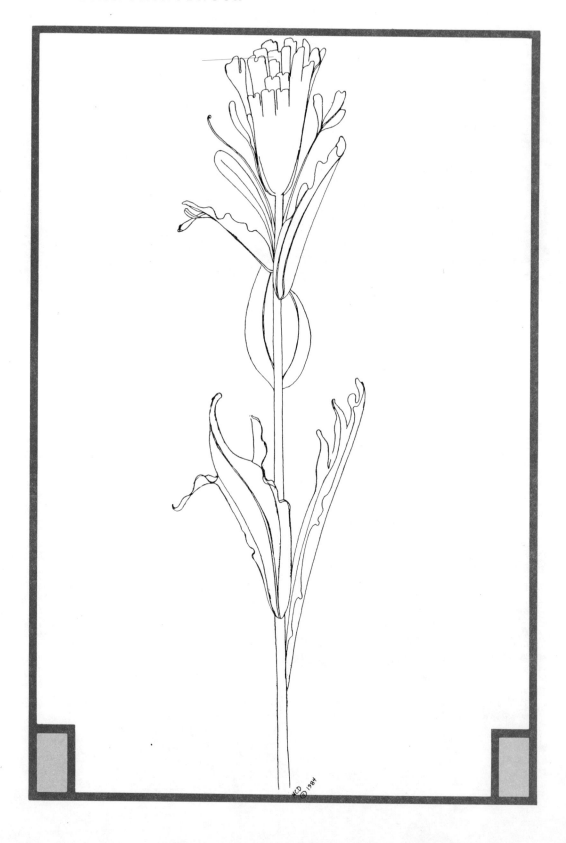

COMMON NAME: **Indian paintbrush**
FAMILY: Scrophulariaceae (Snapdragon)
GENUS: *Castilleja*
SPECIES: *coccinea*

DESCRIPTION: The small flowers of this species are not readily noticeable because they are hidden in the axils of the bright red-tipped bracts, which are most conspicuous. There is a cluster of leaves in a basal rosette, and the stem leaves are sessile and sharply lobed. The plant grows to a height of one to two feet.

HABITAT: prairies and roadsides in moist, sandy soils

BLOOMS: April through August

A legend tells of an Indian brave who was trying to paint a picture of the sunset with his warpaints. Frustrated because he could not capture the wonderfully vibrant colors, he asked the Great Spirit for help. The Great Spirit gave him paintbrushes dripping with the colors of the sunset, which the brave used and then threw away. Wherever these brushes landed, there grows this plant.

The red-tipped bracts are the most outstanding feature of Indian paintbrush, for the true flowers are very small. The plant is parasitic on the roots of other plants, especially sagebrush.

The genus name is from a Spanish botanist, Domingo Castillejo. It is also known by the common name, scarlet painted cup.

According to the doctrine of signatures, Indian paintbrush was used to soothe burned skin and to ease the burning sting of the centipede. Indian women drank a concoction made from the roots to dry up menstrual flow.

A closely related species, *C. linariaefolia,* the Wyoming paintbrush, is the state flower of Wyoming.

MCD
©1983

COMMON NAME: **orange hawkweed**
FAMILY: Compositae (Daisy)
GENUS: *Hieracium*
SPECIES: *aurantiacum*

DESCRIPTION: This plant is one of the few with true orange flowers. It bears several orange dandelion-type flowers on a slender stalk. The green bracts under the flower heads are covered with black-tipped hairs. The leaves are entire and hairy, and the plant grows to one to two feet.

HABITAT: dry, open areas, roadsides

BLOOMS: June through September

Orange hawkweed came to America from France by way of England. It was taken from France to England and was known as French lungwort because of its supposed powers for healing respiratory ailments. Both the orange and yellow hawkweed were brought from the Old World to America because they were used by herb doctors to cure eye diseases.

The generic name is from the Greek word *hierex*, meaning "hawk." It was believed that hawks and other birds of prey drank the juice from the plant to sharpen their eyesight. Another common name is "grim the collier" because the plant is covered with little black hairs. It reminded people of dust on coat miners' (colliers) clothes or of what is known today as "ring around the collar."

Hawkweed is a successful invader, and since cattle will not eat it, the plant can ruin good pastureland in a short time. Not surprisingly, it has earned several uncomplimentary names from cattlemen, including devil's paintbrush, devil's-bit, and king devil.

COMMON NAME: pitcher plant
FAMILY: Sarraceniaceae (Pitcher Plant)
GENUS: *Sarracenia*
SPECIES: *purpurea*

DESCRIPTION: Pitcher Plant's flower is somewhat short-lived, but the leaves will last a long time and make this plant easy to find and identify. The flower is solitary and is composed of five red petals nodding on a leafless stalk above a rosette of numerous leaves. The bronze-green leaves are curved and hollow inside. The plant grows eight to twenty-four inches tall.

HABITAT: bogs and marshes

BLOOMS: May through August

Because bogs have a very low nitrogen content, few plants can live there. The pitcher plant is able to withstand this condition because it is carnivorous, using small insects to supplement its "diet." A sweet substance on the leaf edges attracts insects,,and hairs found on the inside of the hollow leaves point downward so that once an insect lands on the inside of the leaves, it cannot escape. In the bottom of the leaf there is a pool of liquid which contains high amounts of enzymes. Once the insect falls into the liquid, these enzymes help to break down the insect's body quickly so that the plant can absorb it easily.

The hollow leaves of this plant resemble pitchers and give it its common name. It is also called huntsman's cup, side-saddle flower, and Indian cup. The genus was named for J.A. Sarrasin, a seventeenth-century physician and botanist who discovered the plant and sent it back to France.

North American Indians used the plant to cure smallpox and to help prevent disfiguring pox mark scars.

Many species of this genus are considered rare or endangered, mainly due to loss of habitat.

COMMON NAME: **red clover**
FAMILY: Leguminosae (Pea)
GENUS: *Trifolium*
SPECIES: *pratense*

DESCRIPTION: The leaves of the clover plant are dull green with mottled blue tones. The blossoms are purplish pink in dense egg-shaped heads.

HABITAT: common in fields, waste places and along roadsides

BLOOMS: April through October

Clover may figure in more legends and folklore than any other plant. It is a symbol of fertility and domestic virtue and is considered a good luck gift to a woman. It is also a symbol of the Trinity.

Even in ancient times it was considered a sign of good luck to find a four leaf clover. One superstition said that a girl who finds a four leaf clover and puts it into her shoe will marry the first man she sees. Another superstition held that if a girl wanted to know who her future husband would be, the first man to pass under a four leaf clover placed over her door was the man. Another belief was that if a girl swallowed a four leaf clover she would marry the first man she shook hands with.

Red clover is pollinated almost exclusively by bumblebees. The size and weight of a bumblebee make it perfect for pollinating this plant. Each head of the clover is made up of closely packed florets. The pollen is found at the base of these florets, and the opening is so small that the head of the bee just fits inside. While wiggling down to get the pollen at the base of the flower, the bee causes the pistil to spring up. The pistil collects the pollen off the head of the bee— pollen that was left there by the last flower. Immediately afterward the stamens spring up and dust the bee's head with their own pollen, which the bee obligingly takes to the next floret. The bee is so adapted to pollinating clover that when clover was imported to Australia as a forage plant, it would not grow—Australia had no bumblebees. Only when bees were also imported did the clover flourish.

The first record of field cultivation of clover was when the Spaniards ruled the Netherlands. It was introduced into the United States as a forage plant, but is now naturalized.

Clover is especially good as a forage plant

because the roots of the plant are often host to a type of bacteria that can actually put nitrogen into the soil. These nitrogen fixing bacteria can take free nitrogen from the soil and store it in their bodies. The bacteria collect to form bumps or nodules on the roots of the clover and change the nitrogen into a usable form.

Clover blossoms were used as a cough medicine, and old country folk used to drink clover tea to improve the texture of finger and toe nails. The tea was also drunk to thin and purify the blood. A poultice made from the blossoms was used to help cure athlete's foot. The blossoms were used to make a passable country wine, to flavor cheese and tobacco, and to keep moths away from furs in storage.

Almost all types of wildlife eat the clover, including bears, beavers, rabbits, and raccoons.

It is the state flower of Vermont.

COMMON NAME: **sheep sorrel**
FAMILY: Polygonaceae (Buckwheat)
GENUS: *Rumex*
SPECIES: *acetosella*

DESCRIPTION: This plant is characterized by a spike of very small, reddish flowers. The leaves are small, only two inches long, and entire. The plant grows to a height of six to twelve inches.

HABITAT: roadsides and open areas

BLOOMS: June through October

Both the species name and the common name come from the fact that there is a lemonish taste to the leaves. *Acetosella* means "slightly acid" and sorrel is from the French word *sur*, which means "sour." The leaves were steeped in hot water and drained, and the resulting liquid was mixed with sugar and served cool as a woodland equivalent to lemonade. The leaves were also used as flavoring for fish and potatoes and were added to soups or stews as a thickening agent. When chewed, sheep sorrel leaves make an effective thirst quencher. The leaves were also chopped up to add a little zing to a salad.

Sheep sorrel has been used medicinally since the time of the Roman Empire. Horace wrote that the leaves eaten with a cup of wine would soothe a queasy stomach. The leaves were made into a poultice to use on

MCD
© 1993

boils and inflamed skin, and water that had been boiled with the leaves was used to treat acne and skin disorders. American Indians used it as an antidote for poison and to treat sore throats.

Water in which the leaves had been boiled was also used to clean, shine, and preserve wicker and bamboo furniture and to polish silver. The leaves were rubbed on cloth stained by ink to help remove the spot.

The language of sheep sorrel is parental affection.

COMMON NAME: **wood betony**
FAMILY: Scrophulariaceae (Snapdragon)
GENUS: *Pedicularis*
SPECIES: *canadensis*

DESCRIPTION: The leaves are dark green and deeply lobed and resemble foliage on ferns. The flowers can be either red or yellow and occur on short dense spikes. The petals are united, as is characteristic of this family. It grows six to eighteen inches tall.

HABITAT: woods

BLOOMS: April through June

Outstanding foliage and interesting flowers make wood betony seem a lovely addition to a wildflower garden. However, the plant enjoys a symbiotic relationship with a type of fungus, which is found on the roots and supplies nutrients. Because of this, the plant is very difficult to transplant.

The unusual flower has given rise to several common names including red helmet, elephant head, walrus head, Indian warrior, and beefsteak plant (due to the reddish brown color of the blossoms). Another very common name is lousewort—farmers erroneously believed that if animals got into the plant they would soon be covered with lice. Apparently this belief has been held for centuries, because the genus name is from the Latin word for louse, *pediculus*.

This plant is probably only a close relative of the ancient betony that was believed to be so useful and powerful. It was so sought-after that an old Roman proverb suggested "sell your coat and buy betony." An Italian saying was "he has more virtues than betony." A tenth-century herbal

suggested that betony was useful in curing sick elves. It was often planted in church graveyards or worn in an amulet, because it was thought to have the power to drive away evil spirits. Serpents caught in a bed of betony supposedly would lash themselves to death.

The language of betony is surprise.

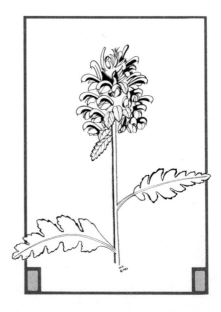

GLOSSARY

anther – the part of the stamen containing pollen

axil – the upper angle formed by a leaf or twig and the stem on which it grows

basal – found at the bottom of the stem

bract – modified leaves usually found underneath the flower

clasping – leaf which completely or partly surrounds the stem

cross-pollination – the transfer of pollen from one flower to another by means of wind or insects

Doctrine of signatures – This theory was proposed by a Swiss physician in 1657. It suggested that some plants had "signatures" to help man know which herbs and wild plants were useful medicines. These signatures were parts of the plant that physically resembled parts of the human body. Whatever the plant looked like was what it could cure. For example, since the leaf of *Hepatica* resembles the human liver, it was thought that *Hepatica* had been put on the earth to cure problems of the liver.

escape – a plant that was once cultivated but has now adapted to natural areas and can thrive untended *glaucous* – covered with whitish, often waxy substance

lobed – indentions in the leaves which do not go all the way to the center

node – the part of the stem where leaves begin to grow

opposite leaves – a pair of leaves growing from the same node, one on each side of the stem

pistil – female part of the flower

pollinate – to transfer pollen from an anther to the tip of the pistil

raceme – a stalk along which flowers grow on short individual stems

rosette – a circular cluster of leaves growing at the base of a stem

self-pollinate – to transfer pollen from the anther to the pistil within the same flower

stamen – the male reproductive part of a flower

simple – unbranched

symbiotic – the coexistence of two organisms to the mutual benefit of both

succulent – thick, fleshy, and juicy

SELECTED BIBLIOGRAPHY

Angier, Bradford. *Field Guide to Edible Wild Plants*. Stackpole Books, Harrisburg, Pa., 1974.

Blamey, Marjorie. *Flowers of the Countryside.* William Morrow and Co., New York, 1980.

Borland, Hal. *A Countryman's Flowers.* Alfred A. Knopf, Inc., New York, 1981.

Busch, Phyllis S. *Wildflowers and the Stories Behind Their Names.* Charles Scribner's Sons, New York, 1977.

Coats, Alice M. *Flowers and Their Histories.* McGraw-Hill Book Co., New York, 1956.

Cunningham, James A. and John E. Klimas. *Wildflowers of Eastern America.* Alfred A. Knopf, Inc., New York, 1974.

Dana, Mrs. William Starr. *How to Know the Wild Flowers.* Holt, Rinehart and Winston, New York, 1970.

de Bray, Lys. *The Wild Garden.* Mayflower Books, New York, 1978.

Duncan, Wilbur. *Wildflowers of the Southeastern United States.* University of Georgia Press, Athens, Georgia, 1975.

Durant, Mary. *Who Named the Daisy? Who Named the Rose?* Dodd, Mead and Co., New York, 1976.

Elliott, Douglas B. *Roots.* Chatham Press, Old Greenwich, Connecticut, 1976.

Emboden, William, A. *Bizarre Plants.* Macmillan Publishing Co., Inc., 1974.

Friend, Rev. Hilderic. *Flowers and Flower Lore.* John B. Alden, New York, 1889.

Gibbons, Euell. *Stalking the Healthful Herbs.* David McKay Co., New York, 1966.

Greenaway, Kate. *Language of Flowers.* Gramercy Publishers, New York, 1978.

Gunther, Erna. *Ethnology of Western Washington.* University of Washington Press, Seattle and London, 1945.

Gupton, Oscar W. and Fred C. Swope. *Wildflowers of the Shenandoah Valley and Blue Ridge Mountains.* University Press of Virginia, Charlottesville, 1979.

Hall, Alan. *The Wild Food Trail Guide.* Holt, Rinehart and Winston, New York, 1976.

Hardacer, Val. *Ginseng.* Holland House Press, 1975.

Harned, Joseph E. *Wild Flowers of the Alleghanies.* Published by author, 1926.

Haughton, Claire Shaver. *Green Immigrants.* Harcourt Brace Jovanovich, Inc., New York, 1978.

Inglis, Bessie D. *Wild Flower Studies.* The Studio Publishers, Thomas Y. Crowell Co., New York, 1951.

Ito, Nanae. *Beautiful Wildflowers.* Hallmark Cards, Inc., Kansas City, Missouri, 1968.

Leeks, Sybil. *Book of Herbs.* Thomas Nelson, Inc., Nashville, 1973.

Lehner, Ernest and Johanna. *Folklore and Symbolism of Flowers, Plants, and Trees.* Tudor Publishing Co. New York, 1960.

Manchee, Fred B. *Our Heritage of Flowers.* Holt, Rinehart and Winston, New York, 1970.

Meeuse, B. J. D. *The Story of Pollination.* Ronald Press Co., New York, 1961.

Muensher, Walter Conrad. *Poisonous Plants of the United States.* Macmillan Publishing Co., Inc., New York, 1951.

National Geographic Society. *The Book of Wild Flowers.* Washington, D.C., 1924.

Niehaus, Theodore. *Field Guide to North American Wildflowers.* Alfred A. Knopf, Inc., New York, 1976.

Palmer, Lawrence E. *Fieldbook of Natural History.* McGraw-Hill Book Co., New York, 1949.

Peterson, Roger Tory and Margaret McKenny. *A Field Guide to Wildflowers of Northeastern and North Central North America.* Houghton-Mifflin, Boston, 1968.

Platt, Rutherford. *This Green World.* Dodd, Mead, and Co., New York, 1964.

Rickett, H. W. *The Odyssey Book of American Wildflowers.* Golden Press, New York, 1964.

Sanecki, Kay N. *The Complete Book of Herbs.* Macmillan Publishing Co., Inc., New York, 1974.

Schaeffer, Elizabeth. *Dandelion, Pokeweed, and Goosefoot.* Young Scott Books, 1972.

Shosteck, Robert. *Flowers and Plants.* Quadrangle, The New York Times Book Co., 1974.

Stupka, Arthur. *Wildflowers in Color.* Harper & Row, New York, 1965.

Weslager, C.A. *Magic Medicines of the Indians.* New American Library, New York, 1973.

Wigginton, Eliot. *Foxfire II.* Anchor Press/Doubleday, New York, 1973.

INDEX

Aaron's Rod, 187

Achillea millefolium, 142

Aconitum uncinatum, 39

Adder's Tongue, 198

Alleluia Flower, 191

Allium stellatum, 40

Althaea officinalis, 214

Alum Root, 210

Anemone quinquefolia, 141

Anemonella thalictroides, 126

Antennaria plantaginifolia, 120

Aquilegia canadensis, 230

Arbutus, Trailing, 83–84

Arctium minus, 17

Arisaema triphyllum, 71

Asclepias syriaca, 73

Asclepias tuberosa, 226

Aster, 11–12

Aster, 11

Atamasco Lily, 84

Aureolaria virginica, 165

Bachelor's Button, 46

Bearbind, 207

Bedstraw, 87–88

Bee's Nest Plant, 124

Beebalm, 223–224

Beefsteak Plant, 246

Beggar's Blanket, 187

Beggar's Buttons, 17

Beggar's Lice, 17

Bellwort, 147

Bindweed, Hedge, 207–208

Bird's Nest Root, 124

Bird Seed, 92

Birthroot, 80

Birthwort, 69

Bitterbuttons, 198

Bitterroot, 88–90

Bittersweet, 118

Black-Eyed Susan, 149, 158

Blister Plant, 151

Bloodroot, 90–92

Bloodwort, 142

Blooming Sally, 210

Blue Bottle, 46

Blue Sailors, 19

Blue Staggers, 96

Blue-Eyed Grass, 12–14

Bluets, 14

Bouncing Bet, 132

Brassica Campestris, 168

Bread and Cheese, 191

Bruisewort, 96

Bullock's Lungwort, 189

Bunk, 19

Burdock, 17

Butter-and-Eggs, 224–226

Buttercup, 151–152, 185

Butterfly-Weed, 226–228

Caltha natans, 185

Caltha palustris, 185

Cardinal Flower, 228–230

Castilleja coccinea, 237

Castilleja linariaefolia, 237

Cat's Foot, 27

Catch Weed, 87

Catchfly, 235

Cattail, 152–154

Celandine, 154–156

Centaurea maculosa, 46

Checkerberry, 116

Chelidonium majus, 154

Chickweed, 92–94

Chicory, 17–20, 171

Chiggerweed, 228

Chimaphila maculata, 116

Chrysanthemum leucanthemum, 94

Cichorium intybus, 19

Cinquefoil, 156–158

Cirsium vulgare, 50

Claytonia caroliniana, 220

Claytonia virginica, 219

Cleavers, 87

Clover, 171

Clumpfoot Cabbage, 76

Columbine, 230–233

Commelina virginica, 59

Convolvulus arvensis, 207

Convolvulus sepium, 207

Coreopsis, 158

Corn Flower, 46

Corpse Plant, 109

Cowslip, 185

Crane's Bill, 210

Crinkleroot, 137

Crowing Cock, 44

Cut Leaf, 137

Cypripedium calceolus, 183

Cypripedium reginae, 212

Daisy, 94–96, 196

Dandelion, 161–163, 173

Datura stramonium, 111

Daucus carota, 122

Dayflower, Asiatic, 59

Dayflower, Virginia, 59

Dead-Men's-Bones, 224

Deadly Nightshade, 156

Dentaria laciniata, 34

Devil's-Bit, 239

Devil's Guts, 207

Devil's Paintbrush, 239

Devil's Plaything, 144

Devil's Trumpet, 111

Dicentra cucullaria, 96

Dipsacus sylvestris, 49

Dock, Curly, 67

Doctrine of signatures, 8

Dogtooth Violet, 198

Duchesnia indica, 193

Dutchman's Breeches, 96

Easter Lily, 84, 198

Elephant Head, 246

Epigaea repens, 83

Epilobium angustofolium, 208

Erigeron annuus, 101

Erythronium americanum, 198

Eupatorium purpureum, 35

Evening Primrose, 167–168

Everlasting, 122

Eyebalm, 179

Eyebright, 14

Fairy Lily, 84

False Solomon's Seal, 132, 99

False Spikenard, 99

Fawn Lily, 198

Field Mustard, 168–171

Field Sow Thistle, 173

Fire Pink, 235

Fireweed, 208–210

Five Fingers, 158

Flannel Plant, 187

Fleabane, Daisy, 101

Floating Marsh Marigold, 185

Foam Flower, 103

Forget-Me-Not, 20–22

Foxglove, Downy False, 165

Fragrant Balm, 223

French Lungwort, 239

Fringed Gentian, 22–25

Fuller's Herb, 130

Galium aparine, 87

Gallwort, 224

Gentiana crinita, 22

Geranium maculatum, 210

Geranium, Wild, 210–212

German Rampion, 168

Ghost Flower, 109

Gill-over-the-Ground, 27

Ginger, Wild, 69

Ginseng, 105–107

Glechoma hederacea, 27

Gloriosa Daisy, 149

Gold Knots, 151

Goldenrod, 175–177

Goldenrod, Blue-Stemmed, 177

Goldenrod, Canada, 177

Goldenrod, Hairy, 177

Goldenrod, Seaside, 177

Goldenrod, Stiff, 177

Goldenrod, Sweet, 177

Goldenrod, Tall, 177

Goldenseal, 179

Goodyera pubescens, 124

Goose Grass, 87

Great Willow-Herb, 210

Grim-the-Collier, 239

Ground Holly, 118

Ground Ivy, 27–28

Ground Raspberry, 179

Gypsy Comb, 49

Hag's Taper, 187

Hairy Stargrass, 203

Hardhead, 46

Heal-All, 28

Heart Leaf, 69

Hedge-Bell, 207

Hedge Bindweed, 207–208

Hedgemaids, 27

Helianthus annus, 195

Hemlock, 156

Hepatica, 31

Hepatica americana, 31

Hexastylis arifolia, 69

Hieracium aurantiacum, 239

Hog Apple, 113

Honeysuckle, 233

Houstonia caerulea, 14

Huntsman's Cup, 241

Hurr-Burr, 17

Hydrastis Canadensis, 179

Hypoxis hirsuta, 203

Ice Plant, 109

Impatiens capensis, 181

Indian Cup, 241

Indian Paintbrush, 237

Indian Pipe, 109

Indian Plume, 223

Indian Tumeric, 179

Indian Turnip, 71

Indian Warrior, 246

Inkberry, 118

Innocence, 14

Iris cristata, 33

Iris, Dwarf Crested, 33

Jack-in-the-Pulpit, 71

Jewelweed, 181

Jimsonweed, 111

Joe-Pye Weed, 35

King Devil, 239

King's Cup, 185

King's Cure, 118

King's Cure-All, 168

Kudzu, 37–39

Ladies' Tobacco, 122

Lady's Ear Drops, 181

Lady's Slipper, Showy, 212–214

Lady's Slipper, Yellow, 183

Lady's Smocks, 137

Lewisia rediviva, 88

Lightning Plant, 52

Linaria vulgaris, 224

Little Brown Jug, 69

Little Pig's Feet, 69

Little Washerwoman, 14

Liverleaf, Round Lobed, 31

Lobelia cardinalis, 228

London Pride, 130

Lousewort, 246

Love Leaves, 17

Love-in-Winter, 118

Lupine, Wild, 61
Lupinus perennis, 61
Lupinus texensis, 61
Lysimachia nummularia, 200
Lysimachia quadrifolia, 200
Mallow, 210
Mandrake, Wild, 113
Marsh Mallow, 214–216
Marsh Marigold, 185
May-Pop, 43
Mayapple, 113–114
Mayflower, 83, 141
Meadow Ranunculus, 151
Meeting House, 233
Milkmaids, 137
Milkweed, 73–74
Mitchella repens, 114
Monarda didyma, 223
Moneywort, 200
Monkey's Cap, 39
Monkshood, 39–40
Monotropa uniflora, 109
Moon Flower, 94
Moondaisy, 94
Morning Glory, Wild, 207
Moses-in-the-Bulrushes, 45
Mountain Mint, 223
Mouse-Ear, 22, 122
Mullein, 187–189
Myosotis scorpioides, 20
Nasturtium officinale, 139
Nettle, Stinging, 74–76
Nimbleweed, 141
Noah's Ark, 183
Noble Pine, 118
Nosebleed, 142
Oconee Bells, 129
Oenothera biennis, 167
Old Maid's Bonnets, 61
Oldman's Nightcap, 207
Onion, Wild, 40
Orange Hawkweed, 239
Orangeroot, 179

Oswego Tea, 223
Oxalis, 191
Oxalis stricta, 63, 191
Oxalis violaceae, 63
Oxalis, White, 191
Panax quinquefolium, 105
Partridgeberry, 114–116
Passiflora incarnata, 43
Passionflower, 43
Pedicularis canadensis, 246
Pepper-Root, 137
Pepperwort, 137
Pueraria lobata, 37
Phlox, 216
Phlox carolina, 216
Phytolacca americana, 118
Pine Tulip, 118
Pipsissewa, 116–118
Pitcher Plant, 241
Pleurisy Root, 226
Podophyllum peltatum, 113
Pokeweed, 118–120
Polecat Weed, 76
Polygonatum biflorum, 132
Poor Robin's Plantain, 101
Potentilla canadensis, 156
Prunella vulgaris, 28
Pussytoes, 120–122
Quaker Ladies, 14
Quaker Rouge, 187
Queen Anne's Lace, 122–124
Queen-of-the-Meadow, 35
Raccoon Berry, 113
Ragged Sailors, 19
Rain Lily, 84
Ramstead, 224
Ranunculus acris, 151
Rattlesnake Plantain, 124–126
Red Clover, 243–244
Red Helmet, 246
Red Puccoon, 92
Redhead Louisa, 90
Resurrection Flower, 88

Rock Bells, 233
Rock Weed, 210
Rockrose, 90
Rudbeckia hirta, 149
Rue Anemone, 126
Rumex acetosella, 244
Rumex crispus, 67
Sagebrush, 237
Sand Lily, 168
Sanguinaria canadensis, 90
Saponaria officinalis, 130
Sarracenia purpurea, 241
Scarlet Painted Cup, 237
Scented Fern, 198
Scratch Weed, 87
Shameface, 210
Shamrock, Wild, 63
Sheep Sorrel, 244–246
Shortia, 129–130
Shortia galacifolia, 129
Side-Saddle Flower, 241
Silene virginica, 235
Sisyrinchium, 12
Skunk Cabbage, 76–78
Sleeping Beauty, 191
Smilacina racemosa, 99
Snapweed, 181
Soapwort, 130–132
Soldier's Woundwort, 142
Solidago, 175
Solomon's-Seal, 132–135, 99
Sonchus asper, 173
Sour Trefoil, 191
Spiderwort, 45–46
Spotted Knapweed, 46-49
Spring Beauty, 219–220
Squawberry, 116
Stagger Grass, 84
Star Thistle, 46
Starweed, 92
Staunchgrass, 142
Stellaria pubera, 92
Stinking Benjamin, 80

Stinking Willie, 198
Strawberry, Indian, 193
Succory, Wild, 19
Sundial Plant, 61
Sunflower, 195–196
Swallowort, 154
Swamp Lily, 84
Symplocarpus foetidus, 76
Tanacetum vulgare, 196
Tanecetum parthenium, 196
Tansy, 196–198
Taraxacum officinale, 161
Teasel, 49–50
Teng-Tongue, 139
Texas Bluebonnet, 61
Thistle, 50–52
Thorn Apple, 111, 156
Thunderflower, 94
Tiarella cordifolia, 103
Tickseed, 158
Toadflax, 224
Toothwort, 137
Touch-Me-Not, 181
Tradescantia virginiana, 45
Trifolium pratense, 243
Trillium, 78–80
Trillium Catesbaei, 80

Trillium erectum, 80
Trillium ovatum, 80
Trillium sessile, 78
Trinity Flower, 45
Trout Lily, 198–200
Turnhoof, 27
Twinberry, 116
Typha latifolia, 152
Umbrella Leaf, 113
Urtica dioica, 74
Uvularia perfoliata, 147
Velvet Plant, 187
Venus' Basin, 50
Venus' Pride, 14
Verbascum thapsus, 187
Vetch, 52
Vicia dasycarpa, 52
Viola pedata, 57
Viola papilionacea, 57
Violet, 55–57
Violet, Birdfoot, 57
Violet, Blue, 57
Violet, Confederate, 57
Virginia Cowslip, 185
Walrus Head, 246
Watcher of the Road, 20
Watercress, 139

Whippoorwill Shoes, 183
Whorled Loosestrife, 200
Widow's Tears, 45
Wild Carrot, 122
Wild Lemon, 113
Wild Lupine, 61
Wild Mandrake, 113
Wild Morning Glory, 207
Wild Okra, 57
Wild Onion, 40
Wild Succory, 19
Willowweed, 210
Windflower, 141
Winterweed, 92
Witch's Candle, 187
Wolf's Bane, 39
Wood Anemone, 141–142
Wood Betony, 246–248
Wood Sorrel, 63
Wood Sorrel, Yellow, 63, 191
Woodflower, 141
Wyoming Paintbrush, 237
Yarrow, 142–144
Yellow Indian Paint, 179
Yellow Star Grass, 203
Zephyr Lily, 84
Zephyranthes atamasco, 84